# WINTER

## An anthology for
## the changing seasons

**Edited by Melissa Harrison**

Elliott&Thompson

First published 2016 by
Elliott and Thompson Limited
2 John Street, London WC1N 2ES
www.eandtbooks.com

ISBN: 978-1-78396-252-5

Page 1: From *Notes from Walnut Tree Farm* by Roger Deakin (London: Hamish Hamilton 2008). © Roger Deakin, 2008. Reproduced by permission of Penguin Books Ltd.; Page 11: © Lucy Jones, from *Foxes Unearthed* (London: Elliott & Thompson, 2016); Page 19: Jen Hadfield, *Nigh-No-Place* (Bloodaxe Books, 2008). Reproduced with permission of Bloodaxe Books. www.bloodaxebooks.com; Page 23: From Reverend Gilbert White's *Journals*, ed. Walter Johnson (London: George Routledge, 1931); Page 26: Adapted from material first published in the *Biddestone Broadsheet*. © Elizabeth Gardiner; Page 30: John Fowles, from *The Journals: Volume 2* (London: Jonathan Cape, 2006) © J. R. Fowles Ltd 2006; Page 42: From *Small Island* by Andrea Levy, Copyright © 2004 by Headline Publishing. Reprinted by permission of David Grossman Literary Agency Ltd; Page 44: Translation © Eleanor Parker 2014; Page 67: 'Failing Light' is taken from *Out of the Valley: Another Year at Wormingford* © Ronald Blythe, 2007. Published by Canterbury Press. Used by permission; Page 69: A version of this piece first published in Eastern Daily Press' *Norfolk*, 2013. © Norfolk Wildlife Trust; Page 71: 'Snow' from *Collected Poems* by Louis MacNeice (Faber & Faber), printed by permission of David Higham Associates Limited; Page 76: From *Black Country* by Liz Berry, published by Chatto & Windus. Reproduced by permission of The Random House Group Ltd; Page 79: Henry Tegner, from *A Border County* (1955), courtesy of the Author's Estate; Page 88: From *The Cherry Tree*, copyright the estate of the late Adrian Bell; Page 91: © Al Alvarez, 2013, *Pondlife: A Swimmer's Journal*, Bloomsbury Publishing Plc; Page 93: From *The Collected Poems of R.S. Thomas 1945–1990* (Phoenix, 2003). Reproduced by permission of the Author's Estate; Page 94: From Reverend Gilbert White's *Journals*, ed. Walter Johnson (London: George Routledge, 1931); Page 95: Copyright © Richard Adams 1985. First published by Viking 1985; reproduced with kind permission of David Higham Associates Ltd; Page 117: Courtesy of Special Collections, University of Exeter; Page 123: From *Tarka the Otter* by Henry Williamson, published by Pelican and Penguin Modern Classics. © The Henry Williamson Literary Estate; Page 137: Copyright © Robert Macfarlane, 2003. Reproduced by permission of Granta Publications; Page 141: From *Yesterday's Harvest*, © Brian Carter. Reproduced by kind permission of the Author's Estate; Page 148: From *John Clare: Major Works*, eds. Eric Robinson and David Powell (Oxford World's Classics, 1984); Page 149: Sheila Stewart, from *Lifting the Latch: A Life on the Land* (1987), courtesy of the Author's Estate; Page 167: From Reverend Gilbert White's *Journals*, ed. Walter Johnson (London: George Routledge, 1931); Page 176: From Clare Leighton's *The Farmer's Year*, courtesy of the author's estate; Page 202 'Light' by Kathleen Jamie, a chapter extract from *Sightlines* © Kathleen Jamie 2012. Published by Sort of Books, www.sortof.co.uk.

Commissioning editor: Jennie Condell. Series research: Brónagh Woods

9 8 7

A catalogue record for this book is available from the British Library.

Printed in the UK by TJ Books Limited.

# CONTENTS

# INTRODUCTION

When we think of winter, we often think of snow: deep drifts of it blanketing our rooftops and gardens, fields and lanes; white and silent and still. Snow appears on our Christmas cards and wrapping paper, despite white Christmases being vanishingly rare; and it looms large in our childhood memories of winter, outcompeting, by its glamour, the more mundane (but far more common) days of freezing rain or louring, gunmetal skies.

Snow is common in English literature, too – particularly that concerned with the natural world. Small wonder, for what a satisfying thing it is to describe, and how useful to a storyteller its transformational properties can be! In selecting the classic extracts for this anthology snow seemed at first glance to be everywhere: shorthand, almost, for winter's lifeless grip. But look a little further and there's far more on offer, from Deakin's 'sharp, sugaring frost' to Barbellion's low and 'luminant' winter sun.

Because winter, of course, means much more than snow, as the sheer variety of pieces old and new here demonstrates. What's more, it's far from lifeless, for everywhere nature is persisting, readying itself for the age-old cycle to begin again. In the trees the sap is low, the deciduous leaves now shrivelled and lost; but life continues, deep beneath the bark, waiting for the days to lengthen again. Many of our summer birds have flown south but a new cast arrives to winter with us, here to escape even colder conditions elsewhere. Some creatures, like hedgehogs and red admirals, hibernate, but others simply slow down for a while, food being less available and temperatures being low. And everywhere – albeit mostly unseen – insects, and their eggs and larvae, nymphs and pupae, find clever ways (including antifreeze!) to survive the big chill.

This book is the fourth in a quartet of seasonal anthologies published in support of The Wildlife Trusts, a coalition of 47 local groups who together look after around 2,300 special places in the UK. They manage them for wildlife and for people as part of an attempt to help nature in these islands recover from its recent, worrying decline. I've loved working on this series, not least for the opportunity it's offered to discover new and diverse voices – and it's my hope that this series hasn't just celebrated our living landscapes but inspired you to get out and connect with wildlife for yourself. Because it's up to us to turn things around now, and we can start by engaging with and learning about the places that we love.

And that means in chilly weather, too – not just on fine and sunny days! 'We cannot learn the story of the year if we read only eight or nine of its twelve chapters,' said Edward Step in 1930, and I couldn't agree more. There's a world of seasonal excitement out of doors at this time of year, so as well as cosying up with a good book (like this one), be sure to make time for everything wild and wonderful the depths of winter bring.

*Melissa Harrison, Winter 2016*

A sharp, sugaring frost. The mulberry is at its best in November when at last it undresses itself. It does a sort of striptease before my study window, lightly letting go its leaves in a light breeze that seems to touch only this one tree after the stillness of the frosty night. The leaves float down in twos and threes, or just a single leaf at a time.

The glory of the mulberry at this moment of the year is in its pool of fallen leaves: pale yellow softened by pale green and buff (the last from beneath the canopy). The pool is a little sea, choppy with leaves. (Each leaf is a wavelet.)

Mulberry leaves feel tough and gleam like oilskin. They are dull green when they fall from the tree, then turn to chestnut brown as they oxidise. Each leaf is serrated subtly and evenly with little millimetre sawteeth, and the veins are the tributaries of a river, whose delta leads down to the stem.

Elderberry leaves pale almost to white except for their veins, which blush a deep crimson as though animal or human arteries, filled with coursing blood.

Last year I made a maze in the mulberry leaves to celebrate the birth of a little girl – for her first visit here, a labyrinth.

Why are park-keepers so keen to sweep up leaves? They are the glory of autumn and surely would feed the ground if left alone to be drawn underground by earthworms and composted?

All the leaves are falling this morning after such a frost. It has loosened them, frozen and cut off the flow of sap, made each stem brittle.

A pair of crows come to the bullace tree on the common before the house and balance on twigs too slender to bear their weight to eat the plums, translucent pearls of pink and yellow, softened and ripened by the frost, their sugars concentrated now. Magpies follow them, then a dozen blackbirds, a pair of song thrushes. A wood pigeon on the hawthorn after haws.

The hazel is dropping its leaves too, shivering now and then in a breath of slightest breeze. Leaves come to earth like birds to a field for grains, or grubs.

Why don't all the leaves come down at once?

The fun of scuffing leaves as you trudge through them as if through a snowfall, the woodland floor turned to a palette with each tree at the centre of its particular colour. (Turner's palette.)

As the leaves fall away from them, the naked branches reveal their lichened beauty. The pool of fallen leaves is a mirror, reflecting the tree as it has been: the whole canopy in two dimensions. Only the skeleton of the tree is left to represent the third dimension.

That is what trees give us: the third dimension in our landscape.

Left alone to cloak the woodland floor, leaves accumulate layer by layer over the years into a deep crust of leaf mould. Walking, or clambering, through old beech or chestnut woods in France and Poland, I have sometimes fallen through the leaf crust and dropped many feet into a soft drift of leaves. These leaf drifts often fill hollows or old quarrying sites for limestone or chalk.

I go for an early swim and notice the fine old ash pollards on the road back to Thrandeston, and on Thrandeston Green. They need cutting too, but who will do it? I must make a map of Mellis pollards. All need attention to survive. And why not start new pollards too, as I have with my pollard willows?

*Roger Deakin*, Notes from Walnut Tree Farm, *2008*

## November (Sonnet XVI)

*The mellow year is hasting to its close;*
*The little birds have almost sung their last,*
*Their small notes twitter in the dreary blast –*
*That shrill-piped harbinger of early snows:*
*The patient beauty of the scentless rose,*
*Oft with the Morn's hoar chrystal quaintly glass'd,*
*Hangs, a pale mourner for the summer past,*
*And makes a little summer where it grows:*
*In the chill sunbeam of the faint brief day*
*The dusky waters shudder as they shine,*
*The russet leaves obstruct the straggling way*
*Of oozy brooks, which no deep banks define,*
*And the gaunt woods, in ragged, scant array,*
*Wrap their old limbs with sombre ivy twine.*

*Hartley Coleridge, 1833*

Autumn's end in the Northwest Highlands of Scotland is electrified with colour and charged by war in the heavens, although occasional snow may dance across the high peaks before Halloween. Glacial airs from the Arctic begin to do battle with warmer Atlantic 'westerlies', bringing storm-force winds and flood rains. They skirmish for position and influence like gladiators in a battleground stretching from the westernmost edges of the Outer Hebrides to the eastern flanks of the Torridon mountains.

On the shoulders of oceanic air masses dark, gunmetal bands of cloud pile in and yowling winds churn the sea into a frothing, roiling, deep green behemoth. Down in the fields by the shore, glowing waves throw themselves at the rocks and tumble through crevices. They shoot upwards in phosphorescent white foam and cascade down in fraying lattices and nets. Despite the noise and fury, despite the buffeting wind, small brown birds hop quickly about, *pseep-pseeping* as they search for food amongst the detritus delivered by the crashing waters. In the nearby sandy bay, waves wallop and hurl kelp, stones, wood and rope in tangled heaps and then reluctantly recede in a sucking sprawl of lace and filigree. At each withdrawal other birds dash bravely back and forth to snatch at shreds and morsels of nourishment.

When polar air sweeps down from the high north the world turns blue, a glacial clarity descends and, seizing the world for itself, encases everything in glittering crystal. Showers then are of ice and hail, shards of stinging wickedness coating the ground in rhinestones and silver. A billion jewels are lit up by the pale sun, reflecting bands of lemon and cream across the fields. Higher on the hills heather is sprinkled with white, so moorland slopes appear delicately stippled as if by the finest brushes of a pointillist. Sunrise on such Arctic days spreads beams of warmth across the Red River valley, tapping on shoulders and knocking on doors, prodding all into wakefulness. At sunset, bright scarlet luminescent flashes pierce the landscape as the dipping sun is reflected in croft windows until finally the sky turns a deep Prussian blue.

Wildlife seems to instinctively know that we have joined the headlong rush to the winter solstice. Those who needed to fly south have done so; others seek out the last, shrivelled berries and seeds in the clumps of bramble and withered hawthorn. Surprisingly there are few hedges in these coastal areas, though the croft has several protecting the gardens from marauding deer, and there is a small patch of mixed woodland. Here blue tits, great tits, chaffinches, green and gold finches and red-breasted bullfinches will seek sustenance in the dark, lean times ahead. Thrushes, blackbirds and small groups of starlings also root about, while the piercing song of robins and wrens are testament to their collective determination and perseverance. In the fields, meadow pipits hide in clumps of rush and tussock grass, while overhead hunters swoop: hooded crows and ravens, raptors including peregrines and harriers, and, high above, eagles.

On the surrounding moorland the large groups of deer separate. Young stags run together in gangs and move down to the valley to steal what they can, while small groups of females pass across the croft to the shore. Here, they nibble at machair grasses, lick salt from the stones and occasionally pick at the seaweed. On the skyline, victorious, rut-blooded, many-pointed individual males stand imperiously, still watching even as their hormone levels diminish. Yet they too will visit croft fields and raid gardens in the coming months as winter waxes and wanes.

Higher still on the mountain tops early snow deepens, first in north-facing crevices, then in corries. It will build quickly here, but can just as rapidly melt away as warm, wet masses of air move in from the Atlantic. It is a fickle time this early winter. Snow hares, snow foxes and ptarmigans perform colourist's miracles, and begin to exchange rust-brown, dun and grey coats or feathers for Hans Christian Andersen cloaks of Snow Queen white, but rapid melts can betray their new whiteness to the hunters. The close proximity of these peaks to ocean and salty winds often prohibits the formation of permanent ice fields, creating conditions that can bring death. West-facing slopes are particularly unpredictable and unstable and avalanches and floods are common. Such speedy changes between freeze and defrost have impact far down-slope too. Meltwaters merge with tepid storm rains and churn downstream to flood burn and loch. Rivers filled with debris turn rust-red and they roar and pulse with light and foam as they sluice down to the sea.

After the Byzantine colours of autumn the landscape begins to seem weary, anaemic and bleached of colour: burnt umber and ashen hills, pale buff grass mats in the fields and trees with grey-green bark and branches. Daylight can be as bland as old dishwater that has lost its bubbles, so everything looks out of focus; islands appear and disappear and sea merges with sky in a single sheet of unpolished steel. Yet even on such wrung-out days there are fleeting moments when clouds part, lemon light cascades across the fields and the world, for a time, glows with the magic of it all. Then the hills are colourfully transformed into Harris tweed coats, grassy fields become lambent silken scarves and trees are gloved with phosphorescing bearded lichens. Nature's drab clothes light up like an emperor's finest new raiment, protecting the sleeping, hibernating life beneath.

Quickly, days shorten; somehow we all adjust and welcome the dark, for it is neither threatening nor smothering. Darkness becomes a thing of joy and vivid beauty in its own right. When early winter storms blow in, night skies are shrouded in heavy swathes of purple-black velvet. On cloudless nights the Milky Way curves overhead, a broad, braided river of light coursing through the sky. And in this time of conflict and rapid change, of life and death, other lights become visible as the darkness deepens: flickering and shimmering in neon greens and reds, the Northern Lights should be ringing with trumpets and other heavenly music as they herald the arrival of winter, but they are utterly silent.

*Annie Worsley, 2016*

The Voice of the Greta, and the Cock-crowing: the Voice seems to grow, like a Flower on or about the water beyond the Bridge, while the Cock crowing is nowhere particular, it is at any place I imagine & do not distinctly see. A most remarkable Sky! The Moon, now waned to a perfect Ostrich's Egg, hangs over our House almost – only so much beyond it, garden-ward, that I can see it, holding my Head out of the smaller Study window. The Sky is covered with whitish, & with dingy *Cloudage*, thin dingiest Scud close under the moon & one side of it moving, all else moveless; but there are two great Breaks of Blue Sky – the one stretching over our House, & away toward Castlerigg, & this is speckled & blotched with white Cloud – the other hangs over the road, in the line of the Road, in the shape of a    I do not know what to call it: but this is the Figure – this is unspeckled, all blue – 3 Stars in it / more in the former Break – all unmoving. The water leaden white, even as the grey Gleam of Water is in latest Twilight. – Now while I have been writing this & gazing between whiles (it is 40 M. past Two) the Break over the road is swallowed up, & the Stars gone, the Break over the House is narrowed into a rude Circle, & on the edge of its circumference one very bright Star – see! already the white mass thinning at its edge *fights* with its Brilliance – see! it has bedimmed it – & now it is gone – & the Moon is gone. The Cock-crowing too has ceased. The Greta sounds on, for ever. But I hear only the Ticking of my Watch, in the Pen-place of my Writing-Desk, & the far lower note of the noise of the Fire

– perpetual, yet seeming uncertain / it is the low voice of quiet Change, of Destruction doing its work by little & little.

Wednesday Morning, 20 minutes past 2 o'clock.
November 2nd, 1803

*Samuel Taylor Coleridge, diaries, 1803*

The sun was beginning to set in the late afternoon as I walked home through the park, and I could sense a change in the atmosphere. Quiet. Calm. Peace. Blood slowing. Hummed to stillness by the wild things, the trees and their roots.

It was prime foxing hour in the city so I wandered slowly down my favoured edge: a tree corridor, ridged on one side by a railway track and on the other by a raised part of the park that provides a welcome, rare horizon to soothe the sensory overload. On my left, there were plenty of potential fox earths: large tree roots, bushes, wallows, banks and dips, a fox's wonderland. I paused in the shadows, hoping, as dusk settled, to see a local heading out for its evening meal. Voles, worms or sandwich crusts, perhaps. Leaves clung to the trees like shreds of scrap paper, tatty and ragged. Flurries of *Clematis vitalba*, or old man's beard, were bent over, grey and furry like malnourished wolves. Winter was coming.

As the final squeals of the local parakeets and the bleeps and the clicks of a robin hushed, I continued through the residential roads, peeking through the gaps between parked cars and scouring the tops of fences and walls – I'd recently seen a fox jump up onto a fence that must have been two metres high.

The rising moon was so bright it looked as if it had been freshly born. As my eyes swept the pavements, I spied something furry behind a car wheel. Could it be? Pause. Wait. Still. Holding breath. A fox sauntered out. The body was slender and small, which made its ears look hefty, as if it was yet to grow into them. Perhaps it was a juvenile. The fur on its neck gleamed white in the street lights and the tail looked soft and hung low to the ground. Because of the size and the fineness of the fur, I guessed she might be a young vixen. She seemed relaxed and comfortable; I hadn't frightened her. She was a splendid creature, and, in that moment, I couldn't reconcile the animal in front of me with the nuisance pest it had been seen as for centuries. [...]

We stared at each other, the fox and I, for a charged moment. Her eyes were a pale bronze and seemed bright and aware. She turned away and trotted down the street towards my house. She wasn't in a rush at all. We walked for a while, her in front, me a few paces behind. In those seconds, I got the sense that we were one and the same, that we were both just animals, mammals, predators, denizens of this earth. As she turned a corner, I gave gentle chase but within a few seconds she had leapt up onto a wall and slunk off into the undergrowth. It was an enlivening thrill, as always.

*Lucy Jones,* Foxes Unearthed: A Story of Love
and Loathing in Modern Britain, *2016*

There is one aspect of the gradual close of autumn and the onset of winter of which the rambler should not lose sight. The feeling that is pretty general among people of the average sort is that the country at this season is a place to be avoided: empty, dull, without any interest. All the pretty things like flowers and butterflies have disappeared; the birds are silent; the trees are bare poles and the woods are damp and gloomy. This is the accepted notion: but whenever you have the chance for a ramble on a fine day, go forth and prove to yourself how absurd it all is. Some of the details of the wail are true, of course; but the general charge is false. We must not expect to find snowdrops in October or blackberries in spring. Everything has its season for display; and we cannot learn the story of the year if we read only eight or nine of its twelve chapters.

Most of the trees have lost their leaves, and because of this we are able to learn something more precise about their trunks, branches and buds. Every kind of tree has its own form of trunk, with a special pattern into which its expanding bark splits in order to allow growth of the woody tissues it protects. Each kind has its own manner of branching; and the branch of an oak will be found to differ from that of a beech as much as the rough bark of one is unlike the smooth coat of the other. So, too, with the shoot- and leaf-buds of each: they have distinctive forms and start at different angles from the boughs and twigs, which affects the plan upon which next year's leaves shall be arranged. Compare the short, thick buds of oak and elm with the long pointed ones of beech and birch. Trees that are the first to put out their simple flowers in the early months of the year – such as alder, birch, and hazel – have formed their catkins in readiness, though these are as yet small and hard.

If you are curious to know what happens to the vast number of fallen leaves that rustle under your feet and form a thick carpet in the wood, turn up a few with your stick. Where they are dry and loose you will find that some are covering small insects and snails that have adopted them as bedspreads to keep off frost. More in the open and in slight hollows they have become matted together with moisture, and between these you will find worms and snails feeding upon them and reducing them to skeletons – the firmer ribs and nerves being left. Some are covered with the delicate white tracery of fine fungus-threads. These are also doing their best to break up the ripe leaves that have finished their work in that form and are now to be added to the soil to furnish food for other plants. Some again show that one or other of the Myxies has taken possession; and though these may be in the early creamy condition, by taking away a wad of the sodden leaves containing them, and keeping it moist, you may be able to see the development to the fruiting stage.

*Edward Step,* Nature Rambles: An Introduction to Country-lore, *1930*

A late November Saturday, and at last there's a lull in the wind and rain. Missing the badger activity of the warmer months I decide to take my chance. As I set out, a half-moon is high over the woods, diamond-bright and shaped like a 'D'. It is my only companion in the darkness; the dog would disturb the wildlife, the children are staying home in the warm, and though my husband prefers to come with me, tonight he's out. Besides, it's only half-past four – it has none of the feeling of risk of a solitary night-walk in summer, when darkness falls late. The thought of walking city streets at nightfall makes me far more anxious – these woods are home to me and I know them well.

I switch on my torch for the wooded footpath that leads away from the village. A new, crisp layer of leaves has fallen today on the sodden layer of mulch. The trees above are all but bare now, except for the ivy that has scrambled to the highest boughs, and the mistletoe balls that perch on some lone branches like nests woven by an obsessive home-making bird that doesn't know when to stop. This must be a particularly exposed patch, as further in the trees still offer some shelter. The path winds its way through the thicket and a startled blackbird rattles a course in front of me, warning anything around that I'm coming.

Stepping over a low wire fence I can hear young badgers keckering and squeaking, presumably at play. I still think of them as cubs, though they will be close in size to the adults now. It's difficult to make a silent approach but the romping noises haven't stopped – perhaps they are running for cover. My pace is slow and tentative as I follow the path along the side of the field. I have a night vision device with me – a small handheld monocular that allows me to see the badgers when it's dark enough. I stop beside the sett and adjust the focus, looking for a stretch of woodland floor that's visible, but the summer nettles are still ankle deep. Sometimes natural vision is best, and I glance up into the trees. A cool white light graces the branches, ghostly beckoning arms that now seem to reach out further across the field. The near absence of leaves elongates them, too, a change that has come about in a matter of days. A tawny owl thinks it's night already, calling with that prolonged, enveloping utterance. It somehow includes me, if only by reminding me that I'm a guest here, that no matter how familiar this place seems, it's not my own. There is something other-worldly about it that warms me and carries with it a sense of hallowed ground.

The tawny owls always seem more expressive through the winter months, though perhaps now more is at stake. The young make their own way from late summer through to November, and need to claim their patch. Does he perceive me as a threat here, an imposter? I doubt it, and suspect it's a more general announcement to all around that this is his territory. I turn my attention back to the sett. The badgers have dispersed now and are probably hiding underground; a soft breeze has picked up, blowing my scent in their direction and my hope of seeing them tonight has come to nothing. I really don't mind – it's the unpredictability of the countryside that draws me, the not knowing what I'll encounter outside of myself. Whatever I chance upon, there is always that peace and sense of well-being that finds me here – what we are meant to gain from nature, if you share my world view; perhaps even what we are designed for.

It's not long before the weather really turns and I'm not feeling quite so upbeat. The winding lanes up to the primary school have begun their annual challenge, and the first car of the year has skidded into the ditch. My son winds down his car window and a sheet of ice still stands, an extra layer of glazing for him to play with.

I take to the woods again when I get home, partly to remind myself why it is we chose to live in this isolated village in the first place, and partly as something of a reward for my first scary drive of winter. I want to enjoy the hoar frost before it melts – in an hour or two the silvered trees and bushes will have returned to brown. There is less evidence of winter's touch the further into the woods I go, though at least it is safe underfoot, the woodland floor being protected from falling temperatures. Birds are flying every which way with the urgency of Christmas Eve shoppers, darting and diving unpredictably. It's as if a sense of panic has set in, yet this will be the first cold snap some of them have ever experienced. I get the feeling they are delighting in it too, their unusual energy suggesting an excitement about the winter morning that's not so different from the children's. It could be the nervous drive we feel when we start a race, the feeling that a challenge lies before us, but that we're all in it together.

As I walk back home through the village the pavements are still icy. The postman is out in his shorts, and a row of sparrows huddle together on an overhead wire, their feathers puffed against the cold. It's strange to see them looking so lethargic when their counterparts in the woods are so charged. But then if I were a bird, I know where I'd be.

*Caroline Greville, 2016*

Orion, one of the most beautiful of our winter constellations, ornamenting the sky of an evening from November to February. It reaches from about 70° to 90° of the equator, and between 20° N. and 10° S. on the meridian. The principal stars are *Rigel*, *Betalgeus*, and *Bellatrix*; of these three *Rigel* is the brightest in this constellation, and *Betalgeus* is the reddest star in the heavens.

*Thomas Furly Forster,* The Pocket Encyclopaedia
of Natural Phenomena, *published 1827*

# *Hüm (noun)*

(For Bo)

*Twilight, gloaming;*
*to walk blind*
*against the wind;*

*to be abject; lick snot*
*and rain from the top lip*
*like a sick calf.*

*To be blinded by rain*
*from the north.*

*To be blinded*
*by westerly rain.*

*To walk uphill*
*in a tarry peatcut*
*and bluster a deal*
*with the Trowes.*

*To cross the bull's field*
*in the dark.*

*To pass in the dark*
*a gate of hollow bars*
*inside which the wind is broaling.*

*To pass in the dark*
*a byre like a rotten walnut.*

*To not know the gate*
*till you run up against it.*

Notes:
*broal:* cry of a cow or other animal; to cry as in pain
*hüm:* twilight; gloaming
*trow:* a mischevious fairy

*Jen Hadfield, 2008*

L ondon. Michaelmas Term lately over, and the Lord Chancellor sitting in Lincoln's Inn Hall. Implacable November weather. As much mud in the streets, as if the waters had but newly retired from the face of the earth, and it would not be wonderful to meet a Megalosaurus, forty feet long or so, waddling like an elephantine lizard up Holborn Hill. Smoke lowering down from chimney-pots, making a soft black drizzle, with flakes of soot in it as big as full-grown snowflakes – gone into mourning, one might imagine, for the death of the sun. Dogs, undistinguishable in mire. Horses, scarcely better; splashed to their very blinkers. Foot passengers, jostling one another's umbrellas, in a general infection of ill-temper, and losing their foot-hold at street-corners, where tens of thousands of other foot passengers have been slipping and sliding since the day broke (if this day ever broke), adding new deposits to the crust upon crust of mud, sticking at those points tenaciously to the pavement, and accumulating at compound interest.

Fog everywhere. Fog up the river, where it flows among green aits and meadows; fog down the river, where it rolls defiled among the tiers of shipping and the waterside pollutions of a great (and dirty) city. Fog on the Essex marshes, fog on the Kentish heights. Fog creeping into the cabooses of collier-brigs; fog lying out on the yards, and hovering in the rigging of great ships; fog drooping on the gunwales of barges and small boats. Fog in the eyes and throats of ancient Greenwich pensioners, wheezing by the firesides of their wards; fog in the stem and bowl of the afternoon pipe of the wrathful skipper, down in his close cabin; fog cruelly pinching the toes and fingers of his shivering little 'prentice boy on deck. Chance people on the bridges peeping over the parapets into a nether sky of fog, with fog all round them, as if they were up in a balloon and hanging in the misty clouds.

Gas looming through the fog in divers places in the streets, much as the sun may, from the spongey fields, be seen to loom by husbandman and ploughboy. Most of the shops lighted two hours before their time – as the gas seems to know, for it has a haggard and unwilling look.

The raw afternoon is rawest, and the dense fog is densest, and the muddy streets are muddiest, near that leaden-headed old obstruction, appropriate ornament for the threshold of a leaden-headed old corporation, Temple Bar. And hard by Temple Bar, in Lincoln's Inn Hall, at the very heart of the fog, sits the Lord High Chancellor in his High Court of Chancery.

Never can there come fog too thick, never can there come mud and mire too deep, to assort with the groping and floundering condition which this High Court of Chancery, most pestilent of hoary sinners, holds, this day, in the sight of heaven and earth.

*Charles Dickens,* Bleak House, *1852–3*

## *November–December*

*Nov. 23.*  The stream in Gracious-street runs, after having been dry for many months.

*Nov. 26.*  The farmers have long since sown all their wheat, & ploughed-up most of their wheat-stubbles.

*Dec. 1.*  Some ivy-berries near full grown: others, & often on the same twig, just out of bloom. Farmer Lassam has more than 20 young lambs: some fallen some days, near a fortnight.

*Dec. 4.*  Mowed some of the grass-walks! Farmer Lassam cuts some of his lambs: they are near a month old.

*Dec. 5.*  Fetched some mulleins, foxgloves, & dwarf-laurels from the high-wood & hanger; & planted them in the garden.

*Dec. 11.*  Planted 4 small spruce firs, & 2 Lombardy poplars in Baker's hill; & one spruce fir in farmer Parson's garden.

*Dec. 18.*  Hares make sad havock in the garden: they have eat-up all the pinks; & now devour the winter cabbage-plants, the spinage, the parsley, the celeri, &c. As yet they do not touch the lettuces.

*Dec. 24.*  A fine yellow wagtail appears every day.

*Dec. 27.*  M^r Churton came from Oxford.

*Dec. 28.*  Ground so icy that people get frequent falls.

*Dec. 29.*  Carryed some savoy-heads, endive, & celeri into

the cellar: the potatoes have been there some days. Red breasts die. Wag-tail. Some sleet in the night. Ground covered with ice & snow.

*Dec. 31.* Ice under people's beds. Water bottles burst in chambers. Meat frozen. The fierce weather drove the snipes out of the moors of the forest up the streams towards the spring-heads. Many were shot round the village.

*Reverend Gilbert White*, The Naturalist's Journal, 1783

It is now December, and hee that walkes the streets, shall find durt on his shooes, Except hee goe all in bootes: Now doth the Lawyer make an end of his haruest, and the Client of his purse: Now Capons and Hennes, beside Turkies, Geese and Duckes, besides Beefe and Mutton, must all die for the great feast, for in twelue dayes a multitude of people will not bee fed with a little; Now plummes and spice, Sugar and Honey, square it among pies and broth, and Gossip I drinke to you, and you are welcome, and I thanke you, and how doe you, and I pray you bee merrie: Now are the Taylors and the Tiremakers full of worke against the Holidayes, and Musicke now must bee in tune, or else neuer: the youth must dance and sing, and the aged sit by the fire. It is the Law of Nature, and no Contradiction in reason: The Asse that hath borne all the yeare, must now take a little rest, and the leane Oxe must feed till hee bee fat: [. . .] The prices of meat will rise apace, and the apparell of the proud will make the Taylor rich; Dice and Cardes, will benefit the Butler: And if the Cooke doe not lacke wit, hee will sweetly licke his fingers: Starchers and Launderers will haue their hands full of worke, and Periwigs and painting wil not bee a little set by, Strange stuffes will bee well sold, Strange tales well told, Strange sights much sought, Strange things much bought, And what else as fals out. To conclude, I hold it the costly Purueyor of Excesse, and the after breeder of necessitie, the practice of Folly, and the Purgatory of Reason. Farewell.

*Nicholas Breton,* Fantasticks: Serving for A Perpetuall Prognostication, *1626*

Pheasants. This year I can't get away from them. I only have to open the back door and the ground takes off almost from under my feet with a great clattering whirr of wings. Four large hen pheasants land clumsily in the neighbouring field with reproachful backward glances, leaving me free to walk across my own lawn again. I feel guilty. Apologetic. 'Sorry ladies,' I mutter under my breath, hoping nobody can hear me. 'Didn't mean to disturb – hadn't noticed you there.'

And so it goes on. Another day we'll look out and there'll be a splendid cock pheasant, his ridiculous clerical collar dividing his russet body plumage from the brilliant blues and reds of his head. He usually stays close to the trees, and walks slowly and carefully, as pheasants do, as if their feet hurt. But whereas the hen pheasants fly off, it's possible to walk within a few feet of the cock bird, who seems to have decided that this garden belongs to him, merely stepping discreetly into cover when we come across one another.

I have the feeling that I ought to apologise to him, too, on such occasions. His regal appearance, that brilliant cloak he wears, and that ornamental headgear, gives him great dignity. He takes each forward pace as if he has given the whole business of walking a great deal of careful thought. His mind is on higher things: on affairs of state, perhaps, or finance, the condition of the world and so on, far removed from domestic trivia. So that when he got up on the lid of our cold frame, tried to walk up it and slithered and floundered about like a learner on an ice rink, I felt it was almost treason to smile.

We have got used to him, in spite of his destructive treatment of our windfall eating apples. I hope I shan't be seeing him hanging up by the neck outside the butcher's in town, where several of his cousins were last week; heads hung slightly sideways, plumage drooping, all the brightness of the colour gone. He must already taste too delicious for his own good, sweetened by all those apples. Like Goldilocks, pheasants (and other birds, of course) go from apple to apple, trying each one. Unlike Goldilocks' satisfaction with Baby Bear's porridge, the birds never seem to finish the one they started before they go on to the next.

On another day a couple of pheasants were strolling companionably about the field adjoining our garden. No, not a brace: a couple. Two brothers, perhaps, or, more likely at this time of year, father and son. You could imagine them quietly discussing the quality of the grass, or even the state of the land, especially after all this rain . . . Their land, of course. You can tell from the way pheasants walk, the way they hold themselves, that it is they, not we, who are the landowners. We only hold this particular piece of the world for them on a temporary basis.

Since voicing my opinion that they own the place, we now seem to have more pheasants than ever before. Looking out on to the lawn from our kitchen window we watched four hen birds coming down to the bird table to have a chat and a snack together, much as we might share a coffee with a couple of friends. They scratched at the grass rather like chickens do (not doing it any good at all). One of them then caught sight of the peanut cage hanging from the bar of our rustic bird table, head high to the bird. It looked – or perhaps smelled – interesting. So she strolled over to it and gave it a smart peck. The peanut cage swung away and then, to the bird's astonishment, swung back into the attack. The pheasant leapt back in surprise, then tried again, with the same response from the cage. She retired, having completely lost face, while the other three looked on with what can only be described as 'I told you so!' expressions.

A day or two later, and rather to our surprise, they were back – and went through the same routine again. Perhaps it was a different hen taking the 'let me show you' line. But the result was the same. The cock pheasant strolled by later, scratched around for bits on the ground and completely ignored the peanut cage itself.

Not so the great spotted woodpecker, who took a day or two to work out how to feed from the same cage hanging from our bird table. One claw on to the rough surface of the post, one to hold the container still – or fairly still. Smaller birds stand clear if you don't want to be drilled full of holes.

We watched this same woodpecker at work on one of the big apple trees. It was quite a pleasure at first to see such a comparatively unusual visitor to the garden, but after a while his appeal began to wear off. Apart from the fact that I'm told he and his wife are quite happy to help themselves to other birds' nestlings when the opportunity offers (admittedly not a prospect at the moment), we didn't particularly reckon on turning the bird table into a woodpecker feeding station. After all, he can get his titbits from the parts that other birds can't reach, even if it is obviously easier for him to head for the hanging supply at the bird table.

Watching him tackle his prey in the apple tree, though, made us wince for the tree. We had no idea until this winter how much bark comes flying off in great slices from the blows of that power drill of a beak. Our only hope is that his efforts may be reducing the pest population, and doing next summer's apple crop a good turn.

*Elizabeth Gardiner, 1995*

### Sonnet 97

How like a winter hath my absence been
From thee, the pleasure of the fleeting year!
What freezings have I felt, what dark days seen!
What old December's bareness every where!
And yet this time remov'd was summer's time,
The teeming autumn, big with rich increase,
Bearing the wanton burden of the prime,
Like widow'd wombs after their lords' decease:
Yet this abundant issue seem'd to me
But hope of orphans and unfather'd fruit;
For summer and his pleasures wait on thee,
And, thou away, the very birds are mute;
    Or if they sing, 'tis with so dull a cheer
    That leaves look pale, dreading the winter's near.

*William Shakespeare, published 1609*

The purity of the sun here: white, silver, gold. I have never been more conscious of it. And how the sea changes in texture, colour, transparency – especially the first. If the waves run from the west they catch in the evening a kind of imperceptible brownish glaze on the westward slopes; the eastward are a glaucous grey-green. Very much the soft light in early aquatints.

Boredom with books, talk about ideas and books, trends and cultures, the intellectual life of our day; it is like a flood, a natural disaster. So many voices. Finally they blend in a universal scream.

Rats: they come round the back door at night and when we come out, blinded by the light, they cannon off the walls and take all the wrong exits. I could have killed one the other night. But even a rat has a right to live.

Underhill Farm, Lyme Regis, 5 December 1965

*John Fowles,* The Journals, Volume 2, 2006

By the time I head out into the university gardens it is well into the afternoon, but there's still a light covering of frost where the grass is shaded by a long, squared-off conifer hedge. The soles of my boots leave perfect melted footsteps on the lawn, transferring the cold into my feet while my head remains pleasantly warmed by the winter sun. Not so many weeks ago the air in the gardens was criss-crossed by the flights of small insects, and hoverflies and aimless end-of-season wasps sprawled over the last autumn flowers. While birds become more visible in the winter, whether small birds on garden feeding stations or wintering wildfowl concentrated after a freeze into small patches of open water, insects perform a great vanishing act. They almost literally melt into the scenery. Today, a superficial glance at the winter garden gives no hint of insect life.

They're still out there, though. Insects don't simply pop out of existence at the end of each summer and nor do many species migrate. Instead, in myriad ways, they pass the winter largely static and unnoticed. Eggs laid by adults earlier in the year wait winter out before hatching in spring, an incredibly tenuous and fragile existence. Others cling on as larvae, often in the soil, where they can descend out of the reach of the coldest temperatures. Some go one step further, pupating to spend the winter primed for that perfect moment when conditions allow them to complete their metamorphosis.

It all adds up to a vast quantity of still life or indeed still lives, millions upon millions of individual insects present all around us in eerily unobtrusive fashion. The winter landscape is not a dead one but a starkly beautiful freeze-frame, life in ultimate slow motion. And it needn't be a dull time for entomologists, otherwise condemned to months of staring wistfully out of a fogged-up window while chain-drinking tea. There are some hardy insect species that pass the riskiest season as adult animals; and there are a handful of very good habitats in which to look for them.

Take, for example, the conifer hedge I'm walking towards and the ring of ornamental cypresses beyond. They're a welcome splash of colour in an otherwise brown, bare garden, not just for our eyes but for hosts of insects that see out the season in the dense shelter of evergreen branches. Observing the insects concealed within the foliage of trees relies on a simple trick, one that seems a bit rude to the poor hibernating creatures: I have come equipped with a beating tray – a canvas sheet stretched over a folding wooden frame. I manoeuvre this up against the nearest hedge and give the branches a few sharp taps with a stout stick.

Insects, slightly dazed, begin to fall on to the fabric and crawl about. Most of them are minuscule: black chironomid midges with fantastical bottlebrush antennae, pale green leafhoppers that spring away from the branch in great clouds, ponderous barkflies – curious insects with bulging faces, classic bug-eyes and translucent wings – and some scrappy little silver darts otherwise known as apple leaf miner moths. All, at most, four millimetres long.

Moving on from the network of ornamental hedges, I come to the cypress circle. Here, the trees are hosting more eye-catching specimens. The pointy-headed bugs in striking red and black livery are *Corizus hyoscyami*, one of the scentless plant bugs in the family Rhopalidae. It's a more common family in Europe; within the UK, this particular species only used to occur on the south coast. Now, it's found in Yorkshire: a sign of climate change progressing steadily north on six legs. *Corizus* is just using the cypress for winter shelter, while the next bug that falls into my tray, a juniper shieldbug, is also here for year-round food. It's a predominantly green insect about the size of your little fingernail, with two boomerangs of cherry pink adorning its heraldically shaped body. As the name suggests, it used to be found only on juniper. Now, though, they're also eating their way through Lawson's cypresses in gardens, and the population has flourished. Similar host-plant switches have proved successful for box bugs and the brown argus butterfly, and are potentially another more complex sign of climate change in action.

Conifers, even native species, are generally considered poor for wildlife, but the assemblage of species on these garden specimens tell many stories. And they are symbolically important plants, too. As Christmas approaches we bring conifers indoors, and some of these same insects become unwitting festive guests in our homes, a kind of six-legged angelic host which is probably not universally welcomed. This is a shame; for the last two years we've had young Scots pines felled during heath clearance as our Christmas trees, and the set of beasts that arrived home with them were to me more fascinating, beautiful and imbued with meaning than any artificial ornament. Give me pine weevils over baubles any day.

I won't be taking any of the university garden cypresses home to adorn our living room, but for this insect lover they better fulfil the function of a Yule tree if left green and growing, a symbol of the eternal life of insects. For now I shake the last few specimens off my tray, fold it up and step back into the diminishing sunlight.

*Chris Foster, 2016*

Coming like a white wall the rain reaches me, and in an instant everything is gone from sight that is more than ten yards distant. The narrow upland road is beaten to a darker hue, and two runnels of water rush along at the sides, where, when the chalk-laden streamlets dry, blue splinters of flint will be exposed in the channels. For a moment the air seems driven away by the sudden pressure, and I catch my breath and stand still with one shoulder forward to receive the blow. Hiss, the land shudders under the cold onslaught; hiss, and on the blast goes, and the sound with it, for the very fury of the rain, after the first second, drowns its own noise. There is not a single creature visible, the low and stunted hedgerows, bare of leaf, could conceal nothing; the rain passes straight through to the ground. Crooked and gnarled, the bushes are locked together as if in no other way could they hold themselves against the gales. Such little grass as there is on the mounds is thin and short, and could not hide a mouse. There is no finch, sparrow, thrush, blackbird. As the wave of rain passes over and leaves a hollow between the waters, that which has gone and that to come, the ploughed lands on either side are seen to be equally bare. In furrows full of water, a hare would not sit, nor partridge run; the larks, the patient larks which endure almost everything, even they have gone. Furrow on furrow with flints dotted on their slopes, and chalk lumps, that is all. The cold earth gives no sweet petal of flower, nor can any bud of thought or bloom of imagination start forth in the mind. But step by step, forcing a way through the rain and over the ridge, I find a small and stunted copse down in the next hollow. It is rather a wide hedge than a copse, and stands by the road in the corner of a field. The boughs are bare; still they break the storm, and it is a relief to wait a while there and rest. After a minute or so the eye gets accustomed to the branches and finds a line of sight through the narrow end of the copse. Within twenty yards – just outside the copse – there are a number of lapwings, dispersed about the furrows. One runs a few feet forward and picks something from the ground; another runs in the same manner to one side; a third rushes in still a third direction. Their crests, their green-tinted wings, and white breasts are not disarranged by the torrent. Something in the style of the birds recalls the wagtail, though they are so much larger. Beyond these are half a dozen more, and in a straggling line others extend out into the field. They have found some slight shelter here from the sweeping of the rain and wind, and are not obliged to face it as in the open. Minutely searching every clod they gather their food in imperceptible items from the surface.

Sodden leaves lie in the furrows along the side of the copse; broken and decaying burdocks still uphold their jagged stems, but will be soaked away by degrees; dank grasses droop outwards! the red seed of a dock is all that remains of the berries and fruit, the seeds and grain of autumn. Like the hedge, the copse is vacant. Nothing moves within, watch as carefully as I may. The boughs are blackened by wet and would touch cold. From the grasses to the branches there is nothing any one would like to handle, and I stand apart even from the bush that keeps away the rain. The green plovers are the only things of life that save the earth from utter loneliness. Heavily as the rain may fall, cold as the saturated wind may blow, the plovers remind us of the beauty of shape, colour, and animation. They seem too slender to withstand the blast – they should have gone with the swallows – too delicate for these rude hours; yet they alone face them.

Once more the wave of rain has passed, and yonder the hills appear; these are but uplands. The nearest and highest has a green rampart, visible for a moment against the dark sky, and then again wrapped in a toga of misty cloud. So the chilled Roman drew his toga around him in ancient days as from that spot he looked wistfully southwards and thought of Italy. Wee-ah-wee! Some chance movement has been noticed by the nearest bird, and away they go at once as if with the same wings, sweeping overhead, then to the right, then to the left, and then back again, till at last lost in the coming shower. After they have thus vibrated to and fro long enough, like a pendulum coming to rest, they will alight in the open field on the ridge behind. There in drilled ranks, well closed together, all facing the same way, they will stand for hours. Let us go also and let the shower conceal them. Another time my path leads over the hills.

It is afternoon, which in winter is evening. The sward of the down is dry under foot, but hard, and does not lift the instep with the springy feel of summer. The sky is gone, it is not clouded, it is swathed in gloom. Upwards the still air thickens, and there is no arch or vault of heaven. Formless and vague, it seems some vast shadow descending. The sun has disappeared, and the light there still is, is left in the atmosphere enclosed by the gloomy mist as pools are left by a receding tide. Through the sand the water slips, and through the mist the light glides away. Nearer comes the formless shadow and the visible earth grows smaller. The path has faded, and there are no means on the open downs of knowing whether the direction pursued is right or wrong, till a boulder (which is a landmark) is perceived. Thence the way is down the slope, the last and limit of the hills there. It is a rough descent, the paths worn by sheep may at any moment cause a stumble. At the foot is a waggon-track beside a low hedge, enclosing the first arable field. The hedge is a guide, but the ruts are deep, and it still needs slow and careful walking. Wee-ah-wee! Up from the dusky surface of the arable field springs a plover, and the notes are immediately repeated by another. They can just be seen as darker bodies against the shadow as they fly overhead. Wee-ah-wee! The sound grows fainter as they fetch a longer circle in the gloom.

There is another winter resort of plovers in the valley where a barren waste was ploughed some years ago. A few furze bushes still stand in the hedges about it, and the corners are full of rushes. Not all the grubbing of furze and bushes, the deep ploughing and draining, has succeeded in rendering the place fertile like the adjacent fields. The character of a marsh adheres to it still. So long as there is a crop, the lapwings keep away, but as soon as the ploughs turn up the ground in autumn they return. The place lies low, and level with the waters in the ponds and streamlets. A mist hangs about it in the evening, and even when there is none, there is a distinct difference in the atmosphere while passing it. From their hereditary home the lapwings cannot be entirely driven away. Out of the mist comes their plaintive cry; they are hidden, and their exact locality is not to be discovered. Where winter rules most ruthlessly, where darkness is deepest in daylight, there the slender plovers stay undaunted.

*Richard Jefferies, 'Haunts of the Lapwing', 1883*

We were in the storm. The uncontrollable force swirled around us and it was impossible not to watch this formidable, noisy and beautiful display of nature. Our faces were turned upwards towards the sky, and then it began to rain down upon us; a gentle shower of fresh starling poo.

The kids thought this was truly the funniest thing ever, and celebrated loudly every time a splat hit them. I sighed because they were wearing their school coats that I would have to get washed and dried by the next morning. Still, their smiles made it worth it.

A starling murmuration viewed from a distance is a peaceful thing. You can imagine an operatic sound track while the perfect arcs and whooshes are described elegantly in the distance, with cadence and grace. Even the word 'murmuration' sounds relaxing and gentle.

By contrast, we were up high, on the top layer of a multi-storey car park. There was no polite distance. Just a metre or so above us was a seething, raucous mass of birds. I'd guess at 30,000. We could hear the wing beats and their excited conversations, exchanging the news of the day as they swooped over us, a twisting, morphing cloud. They reminded me of a group of primary-school children, just let off the bus on a school trip.

If they were chatty children, the peregrine was the strict school teacher worthy of a Roald Dahl story, hurtling in with stern speed. The group of starlings silenced for a moment, then their swoops became urgent and intense. The group split, reformed and divided again. One of their number was plucked from the back in the confusion, and the peregrine vanished with its prey.

Theories as to why starlings flock like this include to share information about food availability, as well as the safety in numbers principle – not that it quite worked in this case. It is also the sociable preamble to roosting together for warmth.

As dusk fell over the city, the starlings eased away towards a large building, level with the car park. After a few false starts they suddenly landed and the noise dropped away to be replaced by the buzz and hum of a busy city in rush hour.

No one parks their car on this level twice. The shiny paint-work all around was decorated with splats of white, much like the school coats and my hair.

*Kate Blincoe, 2016*

## A Thousand Words for Snow

*When the ice begins to miss*
*the silicon, the coal,*
*the cuticle, the uniform,*
*and your skin's a skittish foal –*

*When the tongue melts the thistle*
*in the berry's mouth like hail,*
*and the fractal folds its kisses*
*in a locket's lost portrait –*

*When the water flecks its hustle*
*with mock and pulse and hiss,*
*and you mix oak-apple cider*
*with amnesia's chrysalis –*

*When every stutter is a plaything*
*predictable as the shape*
*that frost takes on a window*
*or of a heart's beat as it breaks –*

*Then look up from the static*
*scroll of winter's radio,*
*white noise doesn't matter,*
*you're at the station so you go –*

*a scarf of thorns untangled,*
*a caddis shell of gold,*
*a swarm of wings, childish things,*
*a thousand words for snow.*

*Kristian Evans, 2016*

We were billeted four to a chalet at the training camp in Filey in the county of Yorkshire. Pure imagination was needed to see how in peacetime English families could actually enjoy a holiday at this woebegone place. Hubert, Fulton, James and I huddled round the hot pipes after every day of indispensable regimen – like running through freezing fields with nothing to keep out the biting sea wind but vest, pants and the order to 'Keep moving, keep moving,' searing from the mouth of Sergeant Bastard. We blocked up the door of this little holiday home with spare clothes, sealed up the gaps in the windows with old newspaper. Every evening we sat close as nesting birds drinking in the heat that wafted from the pipes. Once James took off his scarf but he was the only one. Could this misery be a portrait of an English holiday? One night that bastard sergeant flew open our door and yelled, 'Blimey, it's like the tropics in here. Get those windows open.'

There was no protest we colour troops could make that would appear to this man as reason. From the first time Oscar Tulloch from Antigua met the sergeant's order to move at the double with an inane gape – provoking the sergeant to moan, 'What the bloody 'ell have they sent me?' – every action we took confirmed to this man that all West Indian RAF volunteers were thoroughly stupid. Eating, sleeping, breathing in and out! Cor blimey, all the daft things we darkies did. We did not know that answering the question 'What is it, Airman, kill or be killed?' with the answer, 'I would prefer to kill you, Flight Sergeant,' would see you up to your neck in bother. And that insolent, annoying Jamaican habit of sucking teeth – so frequent did the custom ring in his ears that Sergeant Bastard ordered that particular noise to be seen as an act of insubordination and treated accordingly. Now ask an Englishman not to suck his teeth and see him shrug. Tell a Jamaican and see his face contort with the agony of denied self-expression. Oh, we were all, every one of us, by virtue of being born in the sun, founder members of this man's 'awkward squad'.

*Andrea Levy,* Small Island, *2004*

## Wynter wakeneth al my care

*Wynter wakeneth al my care,*
*Nou this leves waxeth bare;*
*Ofte y sike ant mourne sare*
*When hit cometh in my thoght*
*Of this worldes joie, hou hit goth al to noht.*

*Nou hit is, and nou hit nys,*
*Also hit ner nere, ywys;*
*That moni mon seith, soth hit ys:*
*Al goth bote Godes wille:*
*Alle we shule deye, thah us like ylle.*

*Al that gren me graueth grene,*
*Nou hit faleweth al by dene:*
*Jesu, help that hit be sene*
*Ant shild us from helle!*
*For y not whider y shal, ne hou longe her duelle.*

[Winter awakens all my sorrow,
Now the leaves grow bare.
Often I sigh and mourn sorely
When it comes into my thoughts
Of this world's joy, how it all goes to nothing.

Now it is, and now it is not,
As if it had never been, truly.
What many people say, it is the truth:
All passes but God's will.
We all shall die, though it please us ill.

All the grass which grows up green,
Now it fades all together.
Jesu, help this to be understood,
And shield us from hell!
For I do not know where I shall go, nor how long I shall here
dwell.]

*Anon., c. 1300–1350. Translation by Eleanor Parker, 2014.*

It is my love of Dartmoor that keeps me in touch with the untamed beauty of nature. Much of the wildness in Britain has vanished, even large areas of Dartmoor are farmed and settled; nevertheless there are still many valleys and tors, wild and beautiful, where I walk and find inspiration.

I live in North Devon and I teach at Schumacher College in South Devon. This gives me the golden opportunity to travel over the moor throughout the year, be it winter or summer, and soak in the wonder of the rocky and rugged landscape of open countryside. Sometimes I get caught in the famous Dartmoor fog. But I am so familiar with the landscape that I am not scared.

Once I leave the town of Tavistock behind and am driving on the B3357 I am relaxed and excited at the same time. My favourite walk is Wistman's Wood. Starting from Two Bridges, I find myself among the yellow gorse bushes and silky brown grass of Littaford Tor. I enjoy the mildly boggy terrain between Longaford Tor and Higher White Tor. The view from the top is stunning and in my solitude I meditate on these granite stones from the ancient volcanic age. I think of eternity.

I climb down from Higher White Tor and walk to Lower White Tor. The vast expanse of sky and the rolling hills around me are as magical as they are mesmerising. I lie down on the soft grass feeling the soft air caressing my face. The sun is looking at me from high above and warming my body – it is like god, wherever I am it is always watching me, giving me light and sustaining me. I am filled with gratitude for the grass below and the sun above.

After some restful moments I get up and walk downhill to the mysterious Wistman's Wood. Dwarf oak trees are surrounded by thousands of large rocks covered in soft green moss. These rocks are the saviours of the trees; there are no sheep, no ponies, no cattle and few humans. No one can attack and cut down these trees because of the rocks. I call them the Guardian Rocks. Slowly and carefully I make my way through the woods, afraid of getting stuck between the rocks and hurting myself. Even though I have been here many times, I am still cautious.

I reach the flowing water of the River Dart. She invites me in, wishing to embrace me, so I take my clothes off and get into the water. The stream is shallow, slippery and stony. It is also cold but after a few minutes I am OK, actually I feel refreshed. The source of River Dart is not very far, perhaps an hour's walk up the moor. I am tempted to go there but I have to get to the college by 6 p.m. as the students are waiting for me for the Fireside Chat. I abandon my desire to head to the source and just enjoy the clean, clear stream. I am in non-verbal but deep dialogue with the flowing River Dart. I listen to the music of running water.

After staying in the water for about half an hour I climb up to the woods through the rocks and walk back towards Two Bridges. The footpath above the Dart Valley is clear, straight, easy and comfortable. From time to time I stop and look around at the awesome, magnificent and benign presence of nature – this is paradise. Nature is my religion, nature is my temple and nature is my god. I feel at home. Aldo Leopold called nature the biotic community. I feel a strong bond with this community. I feel I am a member of it. While the world of politics, economics and industry is studded with crises and problems, Dartmoor is tranquil and at peace; here there are no problems.

Nature is self-organised, self-managed and self-healing. Nature maintains a good balance between calm and stormy weather. My reverence for nature is for her intrinsic value. Some people think of nature as a resource for the economy but for me nature is the source of life itself. I think of William Blake who said: 'The tree which moves some to tears of joy is in the eyes of others only a green thing that stands in the way. Some see nature all ridicule and deformity . . . and some scarce see nature at all. But to the eyes of the man of imagination, nature is imagination itself.'

Driving from Two Bridges, I cross over the River Dart again at Hexworthy Bridge, where the river becomes bigger and wilder. The bridge is old, narrow and romantic. I pass the Forest Inn and drive slowly, negotiating a number of sharp uphill bends, and then downhill to the Saddle Bridge spanning a stream that meets the River Dart. In the winter months I have to take extra care here as sometimes the road is icy and slippery. So far I have been very lucky and have never been stuck. I drive uphill through the scenic and rough terrain to Combestone Tor, where the rocks have been made smooth by rain, wind and time – they are nature's sculptures. The deep gorge of the River Dart below and Combestone Tor above is another piece of paradise. A white layer of frost and the crisp air from the north make the moor even more magical. I circumambulate the tor and remember the words of Shakespeare:

*Tongues in trees, books in the running brooks,*
*Sermons in stones, and good in everything.*

The rocks of Combestone Tor are not dead rocks. They speak to me. I am in a silent conversation with them. I feel their presence. They are animated and alive. They have soul, they have spirit. They have memory and intelligence. I feel it in my bones. Even scientist James Lovelock believes that Gaia, the earth, is a living organism and not a dead rock as previously believed.

Unfortunately such enlightened thinking has not yet reached the worlds of industry, business and politics. They see wild nature as undeveloped at best and scary at worst. Roads, housing, hotels, airports and shopping malls are the symbols of progress and development. We have forgotten the wise words of Gerard Manley Hopkins, who said:

*What would the world be, once bereft*
*Of wet and of wildness? Let them be left,*
*O let them be left, wildness and wet;*
*Long live the weeds and the wilderness yet.*

In our anthropocentric prejudice we have come to think that humans are at the top of evolution. We are the superior species. The rest of nature is there for human use. The task of civilised humanity is to conquer nature for its own benefit. I laugh at this arrogant view of humankind, while sitting in the company of Combestone Tor. Bluebells and bees in spring have their own dignity and magnificence. How can I think of myself as superior to them? I have a realisation that the idea of equality should be extended to include all living beings. I dream of a day when we talk not just about human rights but also embrace the rights of nature.

The second paragraph of the United States' Declaration of Independence is too human-centred. It says that: 'We hold these truths to be self-evident, that all men are created equal, that they are endowed by their Creator with certain unalienable rights, that among these are Life, Liberty and the pursuit of Happiness.'

Thomas Jefferson, who wrote these words, was a great president but his declaration is now very out of date. I would like to replace 'men' with 'all living beings', which means all men, women, children, animals, birds, forests, rivers, oceans, so on and so forth.

Why did Thomas Jefferson not learn from the native indigenous people of America, who talked about father sky, mother earth and all creatures as one family, be they four-legged or two-winged, or be they birds, bees or butterflies, as they are all our brothers and sisters?

That ancient wisdom is as relevant and important today as ever.

Those who look at the world and think of nature 'red in tooth and claw' have got it completely wrong; nature is benign and beautiful, nature creates no tanks, no guns, no bombs, no courts and no prisons. Instead nature gives us food, fruits and flowers.

I pass through the narrow road by Venford Reservoir; clear water, pristine woods, fresh air and warm sunshine. Beauty before me, beauty behind me, beauty above me, beauty below me and beauty all around me – this is my ode to Gaia, which is my mother.

I drive through the village of Holne and then by the Benedictine abbey at Buckfast. Now back into civilisation, with its cars, roads, buildings and pollution. But wild and beautiful Dartmoor is still there, alive and inviting.

*Satish Kumar, 2016*

Redbreasts, commonly called Robin Redbreasts, when they come near to the houses, and with more than usual familiarity lodge on our window frames, and peck against the glass with their bills, indicate severe weather, of which they have a presentiment, which brings them nearer to the habitations of man.

*Thomas Furly Forster,* The Pocket Encyclopaedia of Natural Phenomena, *published 1827*

On the cliffs, the wind coming off the Atlantic is throwing everything at us: rain, sleet, hail and sand. It is both ridiculous and exhilarating. The winter sea still has the last storm in it and when it comes into view looks too close, as if it were higher than the land itself and about to overwhelm us. My husband and I, our three children and my parents all take the cliff steps down through a powerful updraft, past the overwhelmed sea pool and its line of pursed, closed beach huts on to the beach.

There is half a mile of surf. Spectacular green waves veined with a crystal undertow rear before crashing with a seething whiteness between black fingers of rock to fizz on the sand. The swell has built up over some 3,000 miles. A lone kite surfer hangs between Atlantic Sea and Atlantic weather, leaping off waves when they break, working the wind as skilfully as a gull.

The weather is moving fast, changing all the time. Claws of grey rain break to rake through a gold half-light and the squall moves like a huge aerial jellyfish, obscuring then revealing this wreckers' coast of muted blue headlands. Swirling white snowflakes move against a grey mass, turning Lundy Island into a Turner painting. It sleets into the sea; we laugh into our scarves and think about fish and chips.

The sky spits hail and we turn our backs on the sea for a moment. Three paired ravens ply the wind, tumbling to the bottom of the cliff and letting the updraft fling them back up as if they were blown rags. They do it mirroring each other, so one appears as the shadow of the other.

From the beach, the slumped cliffs resemble collapsed bookshelves of stacked and toppling volumes of geography. At intervals there are the empty holes of sand martin colonies and, running out by the rocks, an otter's footprints, heading for the café.

On the strandline, we mistake sea spume blown in suds up the beach for wild birds. Clots of foam roll over the sand with balls of whelk eggs light as air: bubblewrap beach tumbleweeds. But there are birds here – vague flocks that wheel out to sea or skim the surface as vapours, and purple sandpipers on the rocky shore. Oystercatchers haunt the bay, their *kleep, kleep* calls rising above the roar, and their orange, lolly-stick bills incongruous as flotsam.

We dodge between coves to see what the storm has thrown up. Tiny barnacles give some purchase to the slippery rocks and bladderwrack squeezes and pops under our wellies, oozing salt-water slime. Our dog finds a dead velvet fiddler crab, rolls in it and will stink for a week. The strandline is a tangle of coloured net, rubber gloves with missing fingers and bits of wood that lie across the angel-wings of a broken gull – and a dead razorbill. Its webbed feet are tucked under the black and white body as if it were diving; its short, narrow wings resemble flippers, its peculiar bill, criss-crossed and bound with a delicate bridle of white, as if acknowledging it will speak no more.

At Pearce's Cove, a startling, brightly patterned object comes into view. A piece of wood the size and length of a telegraph pole – an old mast or a log from a Canadian forest, perhaps? It is decorated in the manner of a totem-pole, with thousands of long stalks tipped with shells.

Little of the log is visible. The shells mimic puffin bills, blue-tinged white, with yellow lips and fine black lines where the plates overlap. These are suspended from strange, watery stems that extend and retract, the shells clipped to the ends like jewels on Blackbeard's beard. The wet, rubbery stalks seemed to grow right out of the log and off each other, pulsating and very much alive. Some are thick as fingers, some 20 centimetres long. They are part-earthworm, part umbilical cord: translucent water snakes. But they are oddly familiar; curiously bird-like with the dip of each long 'neck' and the triangular 'beak' at the end. The shells move, opening and closing as purple, fronded, feathery creatures push out, unfurling as the fiddle-heads on new ferns.

Goose barnacles. Uncommon, half-mythical and sometimes found on beaches after storms, they have spent a pelagic life rolling in deep, Atlantic water.

Writing in the twelfth century, before we joined the world up, a Welsh monk, Giraldis Cambrensis, noted the creature's goose-necked, bird-beaked featheriness and answered one mystery with another, concluding that they were embryonic barnacle geese that had emerged from the sea where they had disappeared to breed. It was a long time until the idea of migration occurred (or was witnessed) by anyone. That seemed (and still does) a far more incredulous feat.

The tide presses and we must leave these doomed exotic creatures and this wild, spume-swept beach. There is no rolling them out to sea or saving them. How much more we know now, and how little. I can believe if I turn my back on the sea again and walk away, they might hatch and fly up the cliffs with the ravens.

*Nicola Chester, 2016*

## Lux Brumalis

*I*

*I am the trumpet muted*
*the bow unrosined*
*and the fiddle unstrung.*

*I am oblique sunlight*
*pale illumination of*
*a world undernourished.*

*I am the broadcast interrupted*
*dead air, station leeching*
*anaemic, into station.*

*II*

*I am the garnet shock*
*of rosehip on frost*
*the robin's titian flare.*

*I am the icebound babble*
*observed, not heard*
*under brittle silver.*

*I am the creeping metabolism*
*of the trout, wintering*
*deep below the current.*

*I am the heart-chilling scream*
*of the courted vixen*
*the crowing pheasant's boast*

*the snipe's 'peep-peep'*
*defying, folding distance*
*across the whispering marsh.*

*I am the withered husk*
*on the naked briar*
*the sap retreating.*

*I am the fiery Saturnalia*
*the blacksmith spark, rising*
*then extinguished, spent.*

*I am the otherworld*
*beyond the black perimeter*
*of the sheltering blaze.*

*I am the chiselled gravestone*
*of the old year in repose*
*and the muttered obsequies.*

*I am Janus, churlish sentry*
*clinging to yesterday*
*wary of tomorrow.*

*III*

*I am the child yet unfathered*
*the page from a book*
*you read once, forgot*

*but must surely read again.*

*Julian Beach, 2016*

I am Australian, and this is my fourteenth English summer. I'm watching the blackbird hen in my Cambridge garden feed a late fledgling, a damp, speckled handful with black wings mismatched to the rest of him like a kid in a Dracula costume. Everything is wet and warm and draggly and sticky, muted compared to the bright-white, scorching Decembers of the Antipodean summer. I am no less hot, for all that. Contrary like Mary, I long for the crispness of an English winter.

One December morning many years ago, when I was new to England and my sense of it still lived mostly in the pages of books, I found a badger paw in a beech wood on Noar Hill, a chalk hill a mile south of Gilbert White's Selborne. In the summer it is all silver-washed fritillaries and wild orchids. That day its flowers were frost.

It was the first hard frost I had ever seen. Splinter-crunch underfoot, everything frozen together in shifting plates of leaf litter and last season's squirrel-gnawed beech mast, a sleepy woodlouse accidentally unearthed. Everything greyed and glittered, blur-edged with ice-fur, but up close! Miniature icicle stick-people climbing on each other's shoulders to investigate the frontier. Feathers made of ice shards, nettle leaves brought high and mighty with each vein picked out, frozen needles rank-and-file. I long to touch the frost-points, to prick myself Sleeping-Beauty style on the tiny frozen spindles. My hands are hot out of my glove and I try over and over, gently, gently. But no. It feels like nothing, like cold

58

water, leaping away from my touch like the star you see in your side-eye.

I put my glove back on. The still air curls cold in my nostrils. There is something in the softer winter duochrome, the slow green–brown ombre fade that puts an edge on your seeing, a sharpness into your taxonomising glance: animal and mineral, the quick and the dead. The paw peeps claw-wise out of the litter. Not a paw to me yet – I am too far away to see, but I have that feeling, the feeling that seems so old, of having seen something. Closer. Dingy grey toe pads, Nosferatu nails. I lift it away from its leafy barrow. It is just the paw, torn off past the wrist, splintered radius and ulna nudging the cuff of my coat. Frozen prettily out of its goriness, shreds of pink flesh clinging to the bones like crystallised rose petals on an iced fancy. I hold it, astonished, in that way that a thing supposed to be attached to something else is always astonishing. A tuft of sooty fur right in the centre of the palm, paler, softer than the shoe-leather parts the badger once stood on, and I am pierced by this patch of vulnerability, this bit of underbelly in the centre of his hand in mine. Hello, Brock.

It is magical in that way that winter is supposed to be; glistening and sugary and otherworldly, transformed and still, a smack of end-of-the-universe absolute zero in the splinters of ice that won't last the morning. Magical in the way of a story told and retold, Herne the Hunter stalking abroad, rich red the right colour, mulled the right flavour, the corners of your mind furnished with wool and fur, fieldfares and the smell of wood smoke. Folklore rises like steam out of the leaf litter.

It is not that an Australian winter is so tepid, at least not on the south-eastern coast where I was born. Sometimes the dew hangs frozen on the grass and your breath comes foggy and the cold rain has made the air resinous with eucalyptus and you think *brrr*, and you're quite right. But I never thought of an English winter in an Australian July. Somehow the winter itself was never the point of comparison – not the meteorological winter, anyway, when Australia's bit of the globe stands furthest from the sun. It was the rich red, mulled and snowy theme of Christmas that stood for it, lifted wholesale from the other side of the world. So in all the long, blowy summer days of my childhood, robins perched on white-capped fence posts on cards on Australian mantelpieces. Paper snowflakes cut at school decked the windows and tiny flocked reindeer hung on the pine tree in the living room as the mercury climbed past 35 degrees. The plum pudding steamed in a saucepan with a saucer on its head, clink-clink-clink-clink the whole afternoon, puffing almost invisible steam black-ops style into the indistinguishable humidity, cicadas screaming in the peppercorn tree like fat green cigars of raw leaves. A pudding made of the soft fruits of summer, dried and stored for a memory of the warm weather months ago, except that here it isn't months ago. We flamed a dark, spicy confection with brandy while the plums and grapes and figs hung ripe on the trees and the canes were full of sugar and raspberries. We curled up on the sofa in our flip-flops and watched the Wombles wear scarves and build snowmen on the telly.

An English winter seemed the true one long before I ever held the badger's paw.

*Christina McLeish, 2016*

60

What I am now going to mention will, perhaps, deserve your attention more than anything I have yet said. I find that, in the discourse which I spoke of at the beginning of my letter, you are against filling an English garden with evergreens: and indeed I am so far of your opinion, that I can by no means think the verdure of an evergreen comparable to that which shoots out annually, and clothes our trees in the summer-season. But I have often wondered that those who are like myself, and love to live in gardens, have never thought of contriving a winter garden, which would consist of such trees only as never cast their leaves. We have very often little snatches of sunshine and fair weather in the most uncomfortable parts of the year, and have frequently several days in November and January that are as agreeable as any in the finest months. At such times, therefore, I think there could not be a greater pleasure than to walk in such a winter garden as I have proposed. In the summer season the whole country blooms, and is a kind of garden; for which reason we are not so sensible of those beauties that at this time may be everywhere met with; but when nature is in her desolation, and presents us with nothing but bleak and barren prospects, there is something unspeakably cheerful in a spot of ground which is covered with trees that smile amidst all the rigour of winter, and give us a view of the most gay season in the midst of that which is the most dead and melancholy. I have so far indulged myself in this thought, that I have set apart a whole acre of ground for the executing of it. The walls are covered with ivy instead of vines. The laurel, the horn beam, and the holly, with many other trees and plants of the same nature, grow so thick in it, that you cannot imagine a more lively scene. The glowing redness of the berries, with which they are hung at this time, vies with the verdure of their leaves, and is apt to inspire the heart of the beholder with that vernal delight which you have somewhere taken notice of in your former papers. It is very pleasant, at the same time, to see the several kinds of birds retiring into this little green spot, and enjoying themselves among the branches and foliage, when my great garden, which I have before mentioned to you, does not afford a single leaf for their shelter.

You must know, sir, that I look upon the pleasure which we take in a garden as one of the most innocent delights in human life. A garden was the habitation of our first parents before the fall. It is naturally apt to fill the mind with calmness and tranquillity, and to lay all its turbulent passions at rest. It gives us a great insight into the contrivance and wisdom of Providence, and suggests innumerable subjects for meditation. I cannot but think the very complacency and satisfaction which a man takes in these works of nature to be a laudable, if not a virtuous, habit of mind. For all which reasons I hope you will pardon the length of my present letter.

C.                             I am, Sir, &c.

*Joseph Addison, from* The Spectator, *1712*

A puddle creaks and then cracks under my boot. A hoar frost has dripped from the branches but the earth is still lumpen and flecked with ice. The oaks are bare and the grass is yellow beneath the broken skeletons of last year's hogweed. Hawthorn and holly have been picked clean of berries by blackbirds still muted by midwinter. The season is at its lowest ebb, quiet and still, except for a ravenous wood pigeon clattering through a dying ash. It's not the most obvious time to go butterflying.

Aurelians, an old word for butterfly lovers derived from the golden droplets on the chrysalis of a red admiral or painted lady, once spent their winter months pinning and annotating, arranging and rearranging the carefully dried creatures they had collected all summer. These dazzling drawers of colour – clouded yellows, green hairstreaks, Adonis blues – nursed these folk through the darker months in the centuries before living rooms were brightened by television and electric light.

Many butterfly lovers perform comparable winter rituals today, sorting through thousands of digital photos of well-focused fritillaries and blurred browns, which make up the collections of the modern era. More often than in the past, however, there are also real, live insects to pity, as erratically warm winters tempt the elite group of butterflies that hibernate as adults – small tortoiseshells, peacocks, brimstones, commas and red admirals – to emerge from their hiding places on sunny days and futilely seek nectar or mating partners.

In hot countries, the big challenge facing butterflies is how to cope with the dry season. In a northerly place like Britain, their toughest task is to endure winter. Surprisingly, most British butterflies choose to face it as fleshy caterpillars, which seems to us their most fragile form. A few, more sensibly, spend winter inside a chrysalis; a swallowtail can survive even if its pupa is submerged in winter floodwater. If I was a butterfly, though, I'd spend it curled small in an indestructible-looking microscopic case – an egg.

Egg-hunting is my midwinter lepidopteral passion and this bizarre, eye-aching mission has become a kind of cult among many other butterfly lovers. I'm searching for the eggs of the brown hairstreak, an indolent insect of late summer, which is mostly brown with dazzling orange on the forewings of the female. It is notoriously difficult to see as an adult butterfly, spending most of its days basking out of sight at the top of an ash tree. Like most elusive things, it inspires a strange devotion.

The female can occasionally be spied in late summer landing on blackthorn and descending like a curious crab to squeeze a single egg onto a crook of a branch, and it is to a straggly blackthorn hedge in Sussex that I have returned. I stand before it and peer, sweeping my eyes too vaguely over branch and twig.

There's no hint of bridal white blooms on this most beautiful and overlooked of hedgerow trees, but its slender bark bears a hint of purple. Blackthorn is often belittled as scrub, a dismissive word for one of our richest habitats. It sends its suckers marching into fields, so farmers slash it back, and more brutal, mechanised hedge-cutting has made the brown hairstreak steadily rarer over the twentieth century.

I can't see anything on its twigs. Standing still, however, allows the fearful countryside to twitch, slightly, with life. A robin sings in a field maple. A hare lifts its ink-tipped ears.

I take a stem of blackthorn in my hand, and more systematically run my eye along its branch, following each divide. Could that be one? I peer closer. It's just a pale joint in the branch. I take another length of blackthorn in my hand, looking, looking. There's a tiny woven sack attached to the stem but it's too cottony to be a butterfly egg and must belong to another small insect.

I'm starting to hallucinate eggs and turn away, readjusting my focus, peeping through the hedge at two rooks who float down for an amble and peck at the hard earth. Then I focus again on the youngest shoots and there it is, a bright speck, a grain of sugar, no more, pure brilliant white when seen from a distance against the dark bark.

The egg is tucked in a sheltered fork of twig, stuck tight to the blackthorn. I've brought a child's magnifying glass with me. Through it, this speck becomes a miniature world. It's a fat squashed orb of pentagonal cells, covered in tiny symmetrical spines like a sea urchin.

I try to picture the life inside but give up, it is so small and alien. Simply knowing it exists, however, an enigma inside a minuscule package invisible even to those who look at an ignored piece of scrub, transforms my feelings about this apparently empty land in the most desolate of months.

Eight months it will remain here. The blackthorn will burst forth with those miraculous March flowers and most of its leaves will darken to a dull midsummer green before the tiny wedge-shaped caterpillar begins to gnaw a very precise hole in the top of the egg. It will take a long day to escape its strong-walled winter pod and make its way into the world.

The stripping back of this season can be a revelatory time. We can perceive the smallest grains of life which are lost in the noisy joyous tumult of spring. Midwinter is the perfect moment to consider the overwhelming splendour of our world, in the form of one tiny egg.

*Patrick Barkham, 2016*

The old liturgy has St Thomas coming just before Christmas, which I used to find strange, or at least unhelpful, until it dawned on me that what the apostle doubted was the Resurrection, not the birth. His feast has now been transferred to high summer, which makes appropriate those words of Christ, 'Are there not twelve hours of daylight? Anyone can walk in daytime without stumbling, because he sees the light of this world. But if he walks after nightfall he stumbles, because the light fails him.' We are walking in the vicinity of old St Thomas's Day and of the shortest day, and although it is only four in the afternoon, the light certainly fails us. They, the disciples, were walking to Bethany, having just been told that Lazarus was dead, causing Thomas to say sombrely, 'Let us go, that we may die with him.' He then witnessed this dear friend's return to the earth and heard the words which centuries of mourners to come would hear, 'I am the resurrection and the life . . .' This was the real indictment of his doubt – that he had actually seen resurrection, and had joined those who would cry, 'He saved others, himself he cannot save.' But the weaknesses of great men are often their strengths and frank disbelief has done wonders for the Church.

The year begins to close when there is neither twelve hours of daylight nor a perceptible nightfall, just December afternoons. The curtains won't draw because of the Christmas trees. Homing birds leave the cold fields. Cyclists waver and twinkle in Water Lane. A horse and its rider pass – with lights. For the first time in living memory, Alf has brushed the ancient ditch which carries the stream to the house and by teatime it is reflecting the stars. It is ages since this water saw the skies, day or night. David has renewed the concrete cesspit cover, and all in a few hours. I think, how able they are, these country people who, although no strangers to the internet and their videos, remain skilfull when it comes to mending the gadgetry of old farms. Little defeats them and not least among their virtues is their easy return to the old order. Twigs, sizeable branches and fat trunks, cut up, lay in tall piles along the bank. 'You will be surprised what will come up now that we've got a proper clearance,' says Alf. A proper clearance, and not a woodland massacre. Or to use the correct and admirable word, management. We burn the dead brambles and provide a secondary starlight, and pools of sputtering ash which will give off galaxies until tomorrow. They remind me to remind Joyce of the candles for the Carols – but, of course, she doesn't need reminding. 'They'll be there.' And of course they will. It is pitch-black by 5 p.m.

*Ronald Blythe, 'Failing Light' from*
Out of the Valley: Another Year at Wormingford, *2000*

Sometimes in midwinter, between the many days that lurk like cold dishwater or hurl their almost frozen rain on us, there comes a day of clear skies on which the low rays of the sun ooze across the Norfolk landscape like egg-yolk, basting gold the wintry trunks of birches and gilding every thing they touch. This is a day for shelving jobs at home, for donning gloves and woolly hats, for slipping binoculars around your neck and heading to the Broads.

Now, in December at Ranworth, Upton or at Hickling, this horizontal light shines through the glassy berries of guelder rose, setting them aflame. Now the alders crowding round the boardwalk buzz with redpolls, and among them is the single introspective note of a siskin. Now the trees trill with long-tailed tits, twirling like tinsel strings about their boughs. A marsh tit sneezes from deep within the carr and in the reed beyond a Cetti's warbler gives his syncopated plink.

Reaching the reeds you realise you're not alone. A furry, gingery face, black-nosed, big-eared, peers at you from the marsh, eyes glinting in the sun. A Chinese water deer: at home, but not at home here, brought by the vanity of humans but so much a part of these reed-beds of the Bure and Ant and Thurne – so loved – that the Broads would not be themselves without him now.

The deer darts, leaving flooding footprints in the blackish mud, and the reed a silent veil of winter dun. But here is next year's life too. Beneath the mud, reed rhizomes store up this year's energy for next year's seven feet of growth. Low among the wind-whipped stems are the pupae of swallowtails; Norfolk butterflies, which next May and June will float like scraps of scribbled tissue over the still dull reed, dropping to flaming flowers of campion and seeking out the leaves of milk parsley on which to lay their eggs.

But these heady days of May are distant imaginings now, as Christmas comes. The pupae sleep, the reeds rest, and the milk parsley will not be seen for months to come. Winter's colour, blazing on this one bright day, is in the heads of drakes on the open Broad. Velvet green mallard heads, banana-beaked, bowing to dappled females as they have since autumn; tight flocks of wigeon, their pastel pates catching the lovely light; tiny teal crouching under the wrinkled roots of alders, piping quietly to their dusky ducks.

As night comes, a skein of pink-feet yaps above, bound for some safe stretch which the feet of foxes may not reach. Marsh harriers sway lower and lower over the reed, dropping to their night-time roosts. And, as you head home tired and happy, woodcock, driven here by brutal continental cold, burst from the carr into the gathering gloom. Tomorrow the skies may cloud again, but today the sun has shone, and, among these many Broadland lives, you too have lived.

*Nick Acheson, 2013*

## Snow

The room was suddenly rich and the great bay-window was
Spawning snow and pink roses against it
Soundlessly collateral and incompatible:
World is suddener than we fancy it.

World is crazier and more of it than we think,
Incorrigibly plural. I peel and portion
A tangerine and spit the pips and feel
The drunkenness of things being various.

And the fire flames with a bubbling sound for world
Is more spiteful and gay than one supposes –
On the tongue on the eyes on the ears in the palms of one's hands –
There is more than glass between the snow and the huge roses.

*Louis MacNeice, 1935*

Growing up in Quebec, I found the winters brutal. Sure we had crisp, sunny days that put a swing in my step (or would have, were it not for the snowdrifts), and I loved the end-of-winter tradition of 'sugaring off' when the sap from maple trees is boiled into a syrup and eaten on snow cones in the forest. But the extreme cold, the blizzards and the icicles on my eyelashes – no exaggeration there – all left a mark on my psyche. The Canadian winter, it turned out, wasn't so much a season as an exercise in endurance. One day, I tried to get the car out of the driveway and the wheels just spun in the snow. Time to call it quits, I thought. Three years later, I was back in England, my birthplace.

On these shores, winter feels more ambiguous: at times a long, grey sigh or a drawn-out ache, with occasional sharp pains to remind you of its bite. The night skies are perfect for star-gazing, though. And if you're lucky, your loved ones clasp you a little closer. Then there are the short-lived days when the wind briefly thaws into a sweet-scented, benign breeze and you feel a frisson of anticipation.

There's an art to the business of wintering. It's a time to revel in the muddier waters of human emotion and to hibernate magnificently. It's not just the trees, shorn of flowers and leaves and berries, who turn inward.

The truly bright spot in winter, to my mind, is the solstice. I love the way it's celebrated with such vigour. I've long wanted to mark the sunrise that follows the shortest day and the longest night of the year – the release from darkness is something to cheer – but until now nothing quite resonated. I didn't fancy joining the crowds at Stonehenge, nor did I want to rise bleary-eyed and shiver alone.

The invitation to walk with my friend Sue's horses on Dartmoor on that morning appealed, though. The plan was to amble hoof-by-walking-boot to Bench Tor, a rocky outcrop on a bit of land that juts out over the Dart gorge. Ancient cultures were believed to come up on the moor and perform ceremonies that connected them with the deeper mysteries of the earth. What more fitting place for a solstice celebration?

We're few in number and set off slowly, in silence. By now, the night has thinned to reveal fast-moving clouds. Will we even get a sunrise, I wonder? Side-stepping puddles, picking our way carefully around prickly bushes and the boot-sticking muddy earth, we're rewarded with streaks of pink and gold seeping out of the clouds.

A walk with horses is not the same as a walk with humans. They're more connected to the pulse of the earth than we are, in our boots. The horses set the pace, beating out a slow, steady rhythm with their hooves. In the early light, a feeling of solidarity arises between us all, two legs and four.

We approach the tor in a howling gale and clutch each other's hands to stay upright on the high ground. The horses, their forelocks standing on end, resemble punk-rockers, but otherwise they seem unfazed. A hat blows off the edge of the tor and someone crazily clambers over to retrieve it. I feel like a kite about to reel off into the skies and glue myself to the rocks. Over to one side I can see hazy green hills, on the other, the gorge, right down to the Dart. The sky's a pale, luminous grey. Not much of a sunrise, but who cares? I'm here.

One of the horses, William, suddenly whinnies. In the distance, I can just about make out a wild herd cantering towards us. There are three horses, including a mare Sue recognises. Two white, one chestnut. They're like apparitions. We climb down and head in their direction. The gap narrows until the wild horses and Sue's horses are a tentative breath apart. Curiosity and something more lingers in the air.

William and one of his wild 'cousins' begin to nuzzle each other. We stare and smile, soothed and moved by their gentleness. Suddenly, the heavens open and it begins to hail and rain. We walk back over the moor, horses and humans, drenched, muddy and brighter. Now, I think, I'm ready to face the rest of winter.

*Jini Reddy, 2016*

Winter Berries.—The principal Berries which ornament our country on the naked boughs during the winter months are as follows:

The Holy *Ilex aquifolium*, whose berries are scarlet.

Ivy *Hedera Helix*, berries green.

Pyracantha *Mespilus Pyracantha*, berries bright-orange.

White Thorn *Crategus Oxycantha*, berries red.

Wild Roses, *Rosa Canina*, &c. berries light red.

Black Thorn *Prunus Spinosa*, berries bluish grey.

Bittersweet Nightshade *Solarium dulcamara*, red.

Missletoe *Viscum Album*, berries green.

Yew *Taxus baccata*, berries red.

These, and several other shrubs bearing ornamental berries, should be sought for in laying out a garden; they ornament nature when all but the evergreens are leafless, and serve to decorate our windows and churches at Christmas.

*Thomas Furly Forster,* The Pocket Encyclopaedia
of Natural Phenomena, *published 1827*

### Christmas Eve

*Tonight the Black Country is tinselled by sleet*
*falling on the little towns lit up in the darkness*
*like constellations – the Pigeon, the Collier –*
*and upon the shooting stars of boy racers*
*who comet through the streets in white Novas.*
*It's blowing in drifts from the pit banks,*
*over the brown ribbon of the cut, over Beacon Hill,*
*through the lap-loved chimneys of the factories.*
*Sleet is tumbling into the lap of the plastercast Mary*
*by the manger at St Jude's, her face gorgeous and naive*
*as the last Bilston carnival queen.*
*In the low-rise flats opposite the cemetery,*
*Mrs Showell is turning on her fibre-optic tree*
*and unfolding her ticket for the rollover lottery*
*though we ay never 'ad a bit o luck in ower lives*
*and upstairs in the box-rooms of a thousand semis*
*hearts are stuttering and minds unravelling*
*like unfinished knitting.*
*And the sleet fattens and softens to snow,*
*blanking the crowded rows of terraces*
*and their tiny hankies of garden, white now, surrendering*
*their birdfeeders and sandpits, the shed Mick built*
*last Autumn when the factory clammed up.*
*And the work's gone again*

*and the old boys are up at dawn to clock-on nowhere*
*except walk their dogs and sigh*
*at the cars streaming to call centres and supermarkets*
because there ay nuthin in it that's mon's werk,
really, bab, there ay . . .
*But it's coming down now, really coming*
*over the stands at the Molineux, over Billy Wright*
*kicking his dreams into the ring road*
*and in the dark behind the mechanics*
*the O'Feeney's boy props his BMX against the lock-ups*
*and unzips to piss a flower into the snow*
well gi' me strength, Lord, to turn the other cheek
fer we'm the only ones half way decent round ere
*and the tower blocks are advent calendars,*
*every curtain pulled to reveal a snow-blurred face.*
*And it's Christmas soon, abide it or not,*
*for now the pubs are illuminated pink and gold*
*The Crooked House, Ma Pardoes, The Struggling Mon*
*and snow is filling women's hair like blossom*
*and someone is drunk already and throwing a punch*
*and someone is jamming a key in a changed lock*
*shouting* for christ's sake, Myra, yo'll freeze me to jeth
*and a hundred new bikes are being wrapped in sheets*
*and small pyjamas warmed on fireguards*
*and children are saying* one more minute, just one, Mom
*and the old girls are watching someone die on a soap*
*and feeling every snow they've ever seen set in their bones.*
*It's snowing on us all*
*and I think of you, Eloise, down there in your terrace,*
*feeding your baby or touching his hand to the snow*

*and although we can't ever go back or be what we were*
*I can tell you, honestly, I'd give up everything I've worked for*
*or thought I wanted in this life,*
*to be with you tonight.*

*Liz Berry, 2014*

The coast of Northumberland stretches from the mouth of the river Tyne to a point a little above the town of Berwick-on-Tweed. It is an attractive coast to both the marine biologist and the ornithologist. To the romantic it also has its appeal. It is a wild, dangerous, shore, which annually claims men's lives through shipwrecks and drowning.

At times, however, the sea can compare favourably with that of the far south in its colour and breathless calm. Long stretches of yellow sand at Tynemouth and Whitley Bay are equal to any in the world. They are repeated in the numerous smaller bays which dot the coast from Cullercoats to Holy Island.

The sea, to me, is in its most attractive mood in winter. At this time of year the rapidity with which it can change its face is startling. Its loneliness, too, is an added attraction. To stand on the rocky headland at Cresswell, when big seas are breaking, is to experience a rare thrill. To be able to walk along the miles of firm umber sand, from Druridge northward to the Coquet mouth, is a joy available to few of us in these islands.

Not many residents in the country realise that, in the quaint miniature harbour of Cullercoats, near the north bank of the mouth of the Tyne, there is in existence one of the finest sea-water aquariums in the world. The Dove Marine Laboratories are unusual in the fact that the specimens kept there are constantly supplied with fresh water straight from the sea. A high-powered pumping system, with pipe lines laid out into the harbour, maintains a steady flow to, and from, the tanks of the aquariums. When the tide is high the sea water nearly laps the entrance to the building. The Dove collection of sea anemones, or sea dahlias, as they are sometimes appropriately called, is world famous. Many people believe that the birds, fishes, flowers and animals of Britain lack the vivid colours associated with their opposite numbers in the equatorial jungles and tropical seas. This is a myth. The sea anemones of Cullercoast offer a profusion of colour which needs to be seen to be believed. It is astonishing that the grey, cold North Sea should be able to supply such a wealth of beauty from its rock-strewn depths.

There is one tank in the aquarium which is particularly attractive in the colour of its inhabitants. Anemones resembling the dahlia and the chrysanthemum, to a remarkable degree, flower before one's eyes. The waving petals of the sea growth undulate in the clear sea water, adding living, vibrant beauty to the scene. Through the palest of pinks, to the mauves and blues, the eye wanders in admiration. Crimson and ivory-white strike a colour note of their own, whilst umber and yellow-ochre add a suitable background to the vividness of the whole picture.

In contrast to their outward beauty, these lovely marine creatures are disgustingly voracious in their habits. To arrive at feeding time in the aquarium rather reminds me of a lion house at a zoo, without the roars, when the rumble of the meat trolley is heard in the distance. Anemones, to us human beings, are noiseless creatures. To watch the feeding of these sea growths is quite an experience. Anemones are fed on the flesh of fresh limpets still writhing for the rocks from which they are taken. The size of shilling pieces, this sea-food is dropped, bit by bit, into the top of the tank. A keeper, standing above the aquarium on a wooden platform, guides, with the assistance of a long bamboo cane, the slowly sinking morsels within reach of the anemones' feelers. As soon as the creature senses the limpet in its vicinity, it grasps the food and instantly contracts itself into a puckered conical knob. Occasionally two grasping sea dahlias will come into conflict over a tempting morsel. Anemones only require feeding once a week.

Provided one is near enough to the sea to be able to get limpets, winkles, cockles and mussels, these lovely sea gardens are not difficult to maintain. They have, in fact, one advantage over the earthly garden. Anemones, like the old soldier, apparently never die. They are the nearest approach to life everlasting. An examination of anemones kept in confinement has shown that they display no sign of senescence or growing old. They are apparently ageless creatures. In the Dove Aquarium there is a gorgeous mauve and white anemone, four inches in diameter, which has been there since the day the aquarium was started in 1908. Now approaching the half-century mark, it is as young to-day as it was when it was first introduced to the confined but safe life of an aquarium tank.

Anemones are strange, mysterious, and lovely, things. They may start a craze at any time which might well oust the tropic fish from the aquariums of the present-day drawing room and parlour.

The anemone has an additional charm. This lies in its variety of names. Here are some of them – Glaucous Pimplet, the Beadlet, Trumpet, Deeplet, Painted Pufflet, Latticed Corklet, The Crimson Imperial and, finally, the Plumose Anemone.

Apart from these exotic denizens of the deep, there are numerous other treasures to be found on the storm-washed coasts of the Borders. It is my custom, during the winter months, to visit the foreshore whenever opportunity offers. Sea coal, washed up from the under-sea shelves, clean to handle as jet and hot in its eventual burning, can be had for the picking. Driftwood is to be found, impregnated with sea salt which, when burnt on an open fire, throws out flames of yellow gold.

During frosty weather, birds of all kinds flock to the un-frozen shore-line for food. Great rafts or assemblies of scoter duck, many hundreds in number, swim on the water near the tide line.

One wild Christmas afternoon, feeling the need for exer-cise, I went down to the village of Cresswell. Visibility was poor along the beach. A driving rain, and the spume from the break-ing waves, made it difficult to see any distance. Forcing myself against the wind, I made my way northwards towards Coquet Island. Suddenly, above the sound of the breakers, I heard a high-pitched squealing, not unlike that of a piggery at feeding time. Knowing that there were no pigs in the neighbourhood, I tried to trace the source of the sound, which seemed to come from the sea. I had not gone far when I saw a huge black object writhing in the swirling sea waters as they recoiled from the sandy foreshore. It was only then that I realised I was the wit-ness of the death struggle of a stranded whale. Blood gushed from its gaping jaws whilst the powerful tail lashed out, to beat in vain against the swiftly retreating sea.

On the following day I went back to the beach, to find a dead calm sea beneath a cloudless sky. Sea birds hovered above the dead carcass.

*Henry Tegner,* A Border County:
Being an Account of its Wild Life and Field Sports, *1955*

With the dog for a walk around Windy Ash. It was a beautiful winter's morning – a low sun giving out a pale light but no warmth – a luminant, not a fire – the hedgerows bare and well trimmed, an Elm lopped close showing white stumps which glistened liquidly in the sun, a Curlew whistling overhead, a deeply cut lane washed hard and clean by the winter rains, a gunshot from a distant cover, a creeping Wren, silent and tame, in a bramble bush, and over the five-barred gate the granite roller with vacant shafts. I leaned on the gate and saw the great whisps of cloud in the sky like comets' tails. Everything cold, crystalline.

26 December 1910

*Wilhelm Nero Pilate Barbellion,* The Journal of a Disappointed Man, *1906*

L ike the camel in the fable, Wolsey has won, by stages, the right to sleep at the foot of my bed, claiming ever more of the duvet. It has been a few months since his last grooming and he is better armoured than I am against the mysterious draughts of the basement.

Wolsey wakes when I do and trots up the stairs just ahead of me to take up his place on the kitchen settee, watching as I boil the kettle and fry an egg. For once there is nothing in the inbox. Oxford is not always like this in the vacations – academic obligation is endless – but Boxing Day is an exception.

Only halfway through my milky mug of Darjeeling tea, I find Wolsey pacing the kitchen with the nerves of an expectant father outside the maternity ward. Even now he suspects me of plotting to do him out of walkies. A largeish poodle in his prime, he is not made for lazy days in. This has been the deal for many Decembers now. My family in India do not do Christmas, and Oxford is full of dogs that need walks or feeding. For my pains, I get a rent-free basement bedroom and the run of the larder.

My friends dread the idea of an unbroken winter here. I delight in the solitude, the temporary withdrawal from human company quite unlike real loneliness, even the teatime darkness. 'Oxford', E. M. Forster declared, 'is Oxford: not a mere receptacle for youth, like Cambridge. Perhaps it wants its inmates to love it rather than to love one another.' Forster is exactly right. Oxford is most itself when the parental cars have pulled out of the college driveways, the pavements no longer rackety with the din of a thousand suitcases rolling against the cobbles.

The city centre, where most of the colleges are, has the quality, as Jan Morris says, of 'some marvellous dead metropolis, long since abandoned in its valley, and left to rot in the fog'. But Wolsey and I are in north Oxford. The dons have long since been priced out of its Victorian terraces, yet the streets are alive with the secret, curtain-veiled glow of wood fires. You can hear families by the hearth at their games of charades, their prosperity immune to boom and bust. The neighbourhoods resound with the barking of well-fed dogs.

Sometimes we go to the University Parks, Wolsey and I. He pulls hard on the lead for the ebullient first ten minutes, then settles to my statelier pace, pausing every now and then to leave his mark against a railing or a paving stone, always the same ones. They have acquired a borrowed significance in my private geography of the city, these invisible graffiti, urinary palimpsests we cannot read.

The Parks are a little eerie this time of year. The leafless trees acquire a subtle menace when there are no children or frisbees or picnics around them. The cricket pavilion is deserted and the tennis courts colonised by families of Canada geese. I recognise all the other dogs: Beau, Fergus, Benjamin Franklin. I don't feel in the mood for the Parks today. We turn away and head to Port Meadow instead: through once-industrial Jericho, past the canal where the boats go as far north as Coventry, over the railway bridge and past the car park to where road and pavement merge and tarmac gives way to acres of patchy grass.

There are no fair-weather walkers here. The dogs, less smugly middle-class and on the whole better exercised, keep their heads when off the lead. Port Meadow is common grazing land, and has been (so the legend goes) since Alfred the Great gave it to the Freemen of Oxford. The grass is speckled with the ordure of many animals: the cows' flattened tarts, the sheep's blueberry clusters, the horses' hillocks. Wolsey does his business among them, with an expression that looks uncannily like shame.

It feels like the morning, crisp and bright, for a nice long circuit: due north to Burgess Field, then along the railway line to the Midlands until we hit Wolvercote Common where only the very seasoned know how to avoid the boggy bits. Then north and west until we're back along the Isis path where we head back south, past hundreds of houseboats, all well sheathed against the cold. And now we're walking at the edge of Binsey village, on what Gerard Manley Hopkins called the 'wind-wandering weed-winding bank' of the Isis. And now we're on the Meadow again, with a clear view of the campanile of St Barnabas in the distance.

At home, I turn on the radio for commentary from the Boxing Day test match. Wolsey is spent and lies curled up on his settee. By tea time, he'll be ready for another excursion into the cold. If he's persistent enough, he'll get his fifteen minutes of strutting around the block.

The landlady at the pub, smoking on the pavement, will rush inside, cigarette still smouldering, to fetch a bag of greasy treats. The landlord of the other pub, stocky and fond of Gilbert and Sullivan, will perform an ostentatious Navy salute. The manager of the Bangladeshi restaurant likes to bow from behind the bar. The Portuguese lady at the sandwich shop will offer him a cold sausage if he's polite. The Russian Orthodox monks who live around the corner, indifferent to dogs, simply step aside to let us pass.

Today I'm feeling strong. I ignore his pointed hints, distract him with treats and the hedgehog-shaped squeaky toy I gave him for Christmas. I return to my writing desk by the electric fire, which I won't turn on yet, the better to savour the cold. I grew up where a winter's afternoon meant sunny skies and 24° C; jumpers were for when we went to the mountains as a special treat.

By February, I will have had enough and long for spring, when the Isis in Port Meadow is just warm enough to swim in. At Christmas, the cold still feels like a novelty, a reminder of school holidays in Darjeeling when I'd swaddle myself in shawls with only the tips of my ears and nose to tell me it was touching zero outside. The Tibetan lady who ran the bed and breakfast would bring in dumplings and chilli sauce to go with tea, from leaves harvested from mountain slopes only a few miles away. Memory leads straight to desire; I get up to boil the kettle for my second cup of tea.

Wolsey tries harder to get my attention. I manage to resist, keep my attention on the cricket. Tomorrow, he'll prevail. The most you can hope for with him is an honourable draw.

*Nakul Krishna, 2016*

oxing Day comes to be more of a true festivity than Christmas. We watched the village stirring (for the village) late, and going forth on its several pleasures. Some were for the meet of the hounds five miles away at an immemorial manor. These departed, the first relay on foot with sticks, the second on bicycles later, mistletoe in their caps as usual, but also in their buttonholes each some flower that the warmth had charmed to bloom in a sheltered corner of his garden. Later still the hounds themselves went by, the huntsman and whips bright as holly-berries over the green road-grass. The majority were for the meet. It was, a local punster said, both meet and drink to him. Indeed, it was at the Boxing Day meet that the last of the old manorial Christmas might be found. It is centuries since the whole village assembled under the roof of the lord of the manor at daybreak on Christmas morning to partake of his strong ale and Cheshire cheese. But the spirit remains – at least in this railway-shunned corner of the country it did – and as far as times would permit, the great house on Boxing Day made the old gesture. The gate and doors stood open; the hounds and horsemen stood before the templed Georgian façade, and the master of the house was busy going a round of greetings, more particularly among the foot-followers to-day, for the purpose of inviting those of his own village in for refreshment, leaving the gentry to the attendance of the butlers.

It was really a day of duty for the gentry too, certainly for the huntsman and his whips; for hunting clogged by such a crowd as this was but an entertainment for the people, a parade, a fanfare, a picture of old elegance. The hunting men and women were merely pageant players. This was noticeable by the huntsman's dutiful, rather than eager, set of countenance.

Wherever they went the multitude followed, lining the roads, surrounding the woods, and applauding vociferously at a blast of the horn or merest hint of a fox.

As to that, there was always, somehow, a fox at the first covert on Boxing Day, even if the farmer to whom the covert belonged had to assure those about him that there would be, with a wink that meant he had had one carried there in a bag the previous night, and possibly scented it with aniseed to make the run memorable. Too many, however, were as much an embarrassment to sport as too few, for foxes crossed the scent of other foxes and bewildered the hounds. To-day the wood contained three or four, all of which were found at much the same time. The hounds gave tongue at the scent of one, another ran back, and another broke covert in full view of the crowd. So the countryside rang with the pandemonium of people hallooing, some forrard, others back, while gentlemen of the hunt stood in their stirrups, their hats raised above their heads, each thinking the fox he had seen was the one fox in the wood. The foxes, however, doubled back from the cordon of spectators; the hounds, bewildered and excited by the maze of scents, divided into two packs, which the harassed whips vainly strove to reunite, and the run developed into a circus round the great wood.

First a fox cantered past, and was loudly hallooed, then half the pack with huntsman and a whip. Applause. Within the space of a minute the other half of the pack, followed by the master, another whip, and the pink-coated 'field', blossomed out of one of the ride-ways, deployed in hesitation, and then set off in the opposite direction from the first half. Loud cheers. Finally yet another fox appeared on the just deserted scene, apparently giving chase to the hunt. Whoops of delight.

On the whole, I think they are not sorry at the kennels that Christmas comes but once a year.

These were but distant cries in Benfield, whose true Boxing Day music, the tinkling of the handbells, had just begun. They sounded like the infants of those which had crowded the air with rejoicing peals the day before. *That* had been a general acclamation; with these the bell-ringers serenaded each house individually. It was their occupation for the day. Even as they issued forth in a body, another would be setting off a different way with a gun tucked under his arm, a ferret dangling from his hand, and such a gait and so thick deep-blue clouds of tobacco-smoke trailing from his pipe as gave him the air of knowing that the day was his for his pleasure. Younger ones were off in striped jerseys for the football field, shouting and joking, while yet another was pleased enough to sit alone with his pipe and rod on the bridge over the lake. Yesterday the rare odour of cigars floated along the village street. To-day we have returned to our pipes, but luxuriate in them, with Christmas gifts of tobacco bulging our pouches.

I had given Walter and a friend leave to have a day's rabbiting together on Silver Ley. It was a sport that had thrilled me once, but now I had grown out of love with it, preferring to watch the birds that fluttered along the hedges. The chance of the bolting rabbit strained one's attention from so many a moment of grace and light coming so abundantly to add to one's pleasure in a free-wandering eye, that the sharp swift triumph of stopping dead a flitting form was by comparison an imprisonment of the senses.

*Adrian Bell, The Cherry Tree, 1932*

I don't swim on Xmas Day because I don't like crowds and I'm too old to race even fifty yards. Yesterday there were record crowds and also a record water temperature – 46°F is the highest for years – and they also seemed to have got through a record quantity of mulled wine. This morning the place seemed hung-over after its annual binge. No one had tidied away the extra barriers in the water or the extra ladders on the jetty and there was a case of empty bottles waiting to be dumped. All in all, everything seemed frazzled, including the water. After a week of unseasonal weather, the temperature is back up to 46°F (8°C) and it, too, felt a bit frowzy, like the soft, drizzly weather and the irritable families walking off yesterday's excesses. Only the dogs seemed to be enjoying themselves. Frowsy or not, the water helped purge my over-eating.

Thursday 26 December 2002. 46°F

The weather stays spring-like. The clouds lifted and the sun came out while I was swimming, so I took my time towelling off and getting dressed. The birds are suddenly busy, as if St Valentine's Day was already on us. The boating pond next door sounds like the House of Commons in full cry and in Flask Walk a robin was singing all night long. Has its body clock gone haywire or is it having a nervous breakdown or is it just this crazy premature spring? The water, too, feels almost warm. I did my usual stint to the barrier and back, then dawdled around before coming out. My body clock is OK but its thermostat has changed, as if cold water has become my natural element. Maybe it always was.

Saturday 28 December 2002. 46°F

*Al Alvarez*, Pondlife: A Swimmer's Journal, *2013*

## Song at the Year's Turning

*Shelley dreamed it. Now the dream decays.*
*The props crumble. The familiar ways*
*Are stale with tears trodden underfoot.*
*The heart's flower withers at the root.*
*Bury it, then, in history's sterile dust.*
*The slow years shall tame your tawny lust.*

*Love deceived him; what is there to say*
*The mind brought you by a better way*
*To this despair? Lost in the world's wood*
*You cannot stanch the bright menstrual blood.*
*The earth sickens; under naked boughs*
*The frost comes to barb your broken vows.*

*Is there blessing? Light's peculiar grace*
*In cold splendour robes this tortured place*
*For strange marriage. Voices in the wind*
*Weave a garland where a mortal sinned.*
*Winter rots you; who is there to blame?*
*The new grass shall purge you in its flame.*

*R. S. Thomas, 1955*

## *January*

*Jan. 1.*  Fires are made every day in my new parlour: the walls sweat much.

*Jan. 2.*  There is reason to fear that the plasterer has done a mischief to the last coat of my battin-plaster that should carry the paper of my room by improdivently mixing *wood ashes* with the morter; because the *alcaline salts* of the wood will be very long before they will be dry at all, & will be apt to relax & turn moist again when foggy damp weather returns. If any ashes at all he should have used *sea-coal*, & not *vegetable ashes*; but a mixture of loam & horses dung would have been best.

*Jan. 14.*  The wind very still, for so low a barometer. *Footnote.* Foxes abound in the neighbourhood, & are very mischievous among the farm-yards, & hen-roosts. The foxhounds have lately harassed Harteley-woods, & have driven them out of those strong coverts, & thickets.

*Jan. 26.*  Snow on the ground, which is icy, & slippery.

*Jan. 28.*  Frost comes in a doors. Little shining particles of ice, appear on the ceiling, cornice, & walls of my great parlor: the vapour condensed on the plaster is frozen in spite of frequent fires in the chimney. I now set a chafing dish of clear-burnt charcoal in the room on the floor.

*Reverend Gilbert White,* The Naturalist's Journal, *1778*

Determined that this diary should start off with a bit of flourish, I sallied forth on this fine winter's day to see what I could find in bloom. The answer was, quite a lot. Gorse, ragwort, several dandelions, some hogweed and yarrow, a whole lot of red campion (rather washed-out), a daisy (*Bellis perennis*); and, surprisingly, near the stone quarry beside the Poortown road, several ox-eye daisies (*Chrysanthemum leucanthemum*). In a cottage garden down by the river Neb, a laurustinus in more-or-less full bloom, a bush of purple veronica, some silvery wormwood in yellow flower (smelt nice) and a clump of pink *Oxalis articulata*. There was some kind of cultivated heather blooming there, too. But best of all, on the waste patch out-side my own gate, there was what had every business to be in bloom – a good, big patch of *Petasites fragrans*, the pink winter heliotrope. (A butterbur, I note; whereas true heliotrope is a borage.) I don't know a more beautifully scented wild flower. I went down on my knees to snuff it – like F. T. Prince in his poem – and then brought some in to put on the library table.

1st January


To-day I repeated the exercise I performed on 1st January last, and went out to see what might be in bloom. (It was blowing a high gale, but I staggered along in a balaclava, gloves and a heavy overcoat.) Celandines: a lot in bloom in sheltered, wet places. What pleases me here is that they're next year's flowers, not last year's. Also: one dark-red bloom of escallonia in the hedge opposite Knocksharry; gorse, of course, and ragwort (cushag), equally of course; a good deal of red campion; some scentless mayweed; wild carrot; a buttercup and a dandelion; some rather bedraggled moon-daisies; a healthy, ramping plant of shepherd's purse, covered in bloom; and in the cottage garden down Brack-a-Broom lane, a big clump of 'shot' wallflowers. In our garden two daffodils are in bud.

Wild flowers are like pubs. There are generally one or two open somewhere, if only you look hard enough. On that note this diary shall close, with Orion glittering bright and Sirius, near it, even brighter. It's so cold that the fire is burning very crisp and clear. I can hear the sea; I can hear the wind. I'm not hungry or cold or ill. What more should anyone want?

31st December

*Richard Adams*, A Nature Diary, *1986*

## On Winter

What Pictures now shall wanton Fancy bring?
Or how the Muse to Artemisia sing?
Now shiv'ring Nature mourns her ravish'd Charms,
And sinks supine in Winter's frozen Arms.
No gaudy Banks delight the ravish'd Eye,
But northern Breezes whistle thro' the Sky.
No joyful Choirs hail the rising Day,
But the froze Crystal wraps the leafless Spray:
Brown look the Meadows, that were late so fine,
And cap'd with Ice the distant Mountains shine;
The silent Linnet views the gloomy Sky,
Sculks to his Hawthorn, nor attempts to fly:
Then heavy Clouds send down the feather'd Snow;
Through naked Trees the hollow Tempests blow;
The Shepherd sighs, but not his Sighs prevail;
To the soft Snow succeeds the rushing Hail;
And these white Prospects soon resign their room
To melting Showers or unpleasing Gloom;
The Nymphs and Swains their aking Fingers blow,
Shun the cold Rains and bless the kinder Snow;
While the faint Travellers around them see,
Here Seas of Mud and there a leafless Tree:
No budding Leaves nor Honeysuckles gay,
No yellow Crow-foots paint the dirty Way;

*The Lark sits mournful as afraid to rise,*
*And the sad Finch his softer Song denies.*

*Poor daggled* Urs'la *stalks from Cow to Cow,*
*Who to her Sighs return a mournful Low;*
*While their full Udders her broad Hands assail,*
*And her sharp Nose hangs dropping o'er the Pail.*
*With Garments trickling like a shallow Spring,*
*And his wet Locks all twisted in a String,*
*Afflicted* Cymon *waddles through the Mire,*
*And rails at* Win'fred *creeping o'er the Fire.*

*Say gentle Muses, say, is this a Time*
*To sport with Poesy and laugh in Rhyme;*
*While the chill'd Blood, that hath forgot to glide,*
*Steals through its Channels in a lazy Tide:*
*And how can* Phoebus, *who the Muse refines,*
*Smooth the dull Numbers when he seldom shines.*

*Mary Leapor, published 1748*

My five-year-old daughter enters the river first. Elbows pumping and knees lifted high, she dashes in, her excited shrieks turning to loud yelps of surprise as the chill shoots through her. I follow close behind, my feet instantly numb as they plunge into the tannin-brown water. I find myself laughing with her; laughing off the cold; laughing off the decision to go swimming at the turn of the year.

Grinning wildly she turns back towards the muddy beach and my wife and son, who are sitting with their chins sunk deep into parkas – cradling hot chocolate and cheering us on.

I keep moving. Pushing towards the small weir that brings the Little Ouse into the northern edge of Knettishall Heath; my body gasping involuntarily as the water reaches my stomach. This is the slow torture of gradual immersion. I hold my breath and sink down, my shoulders and face tingling and burning with the cold.

I know it's probably just seconds, but it feels longer. Minutes. Hours even. A whole year of concerns, worries and squabbles sloughed off in a bone-chilling baptism of copper water. I can feel the slow pulse of the river moving around me. It is a flickering heartbeat that has only recently been jump-started. Once heavily dredged and lifeless, the restoration of its meanders and flow has seen the return of its wildlife. Further downstream, crack willows have been allowed to perform slow dives from banks now heavily mined by water voles, and the jasmine-scented fish ash of scale-filled otter spraint can be found at the river's edge. In fact, two otters were seen recently at this very spot: lithe ribbons of dark brown twirling together in play, porpoising in graceful humps – Knettishall's own Nessies – before disappearing silently when they discovered their audience.

It was this river that Roger Deakin wrote about with such affection in *Waterlog*, the book that first inspired me to try to adopt a 'frog's eye' view of the natural world; to dawdle and splash among the minnows and sprites; to experience what he described as the 'terror and the bliss of being born'.

Now, though, my teeth are chattering. Standing quickly, I scramble back to the bank, picking my way around heron tracks that I must have missed in my rush to get in. I can see my daughter's own footprint pressed neatly over one of them, her tiny toes squidged between the skinny digits of the bird.

Two dog walkers are returning to their car; stamping their feet in the cold. I can see them looking over as I emerge from the water and take a towel from my wife. I raise a hand to them then sit down on the bank with the children, embracing their narrow shoulders with damp, goose-pimpled arms. They squeal but cuddle closer, human hot water bottles. I wince as occasional icy droplets wind their way from my sodden shorts down the backs of my legs, but I'm happy, waiting for the glow to start – that delicious post-swim feeling that lasts a whole day; an earthy cosiness that makes your own skin feel like a duvet.

*Matt Gaw, 2016*

The Great Frost was, historians tell us, the most severe that has ever visited these islands. Birds froze in mid-air and fell like stones to the ground. At Norwich a young country-woman started to cross the road in her usual robust health and was seen by onlookers to turn visibly to powder and be blown in a puff of dust over the roofs as the icy blast struck her at the street corner. The mortality among sheep and cattle was enormous. Corpses froze and could not be drawn from the sheets. It was no uncommon sight to come upon a whole heard of swine frozen immovable on upon the road. The fields were full of shepherds, ploughmen, teams of horses, and little bird-scaring boys all struck stark in the act of the moment, one with his hand to his nose, another with the bottle to his lips, a third with a stone raised to throw at the raven who sat, as if stuffed, upon the hedge within a yard of him. The severity of the frost was so extraordinary that a kind of petrifaction sometimes ensured; and it was commonly supposed that the great increase of rocks in some parts of Derbyshire was due to no eruption, for there was none, but to the solidification of unfortunate wayfarers who had been turned literally to stone where they stood. The Church could give little help in the matter, and though some landowners had these relics blessed, the most part preferred to use them either as landmarks, scratching-posts for sheep, or, when the form of the stone allowed, drinking troughs for cattle, which purposes they serve, admirably for the most part, to this day.

But while the country people suffered the extremity of want, and the trade of the country was at a standstill, London enjoyed a carnival of the utmost brilliancy. The Court was at Greenwich, and the new King seized the opportunity that his coronation gave him to curry favour with the citizens. He directed that the river, which was frozen to a depth of twenty feet and more for six or seven miles on either side, should be swept, decorated and given all the semblance of a park or pleasure ground, with arbours, mazes, alleys, drinking booths, etc., at his expense. For himself and the courtiers, he reserved a certain space immediately opposite the Palace gates; which, railed off from the public only by a silken rope, became at once the centre of the most brilliant society in England. Great statesman, in their beards and ruffs, despatched affairs of state under the crimson awning of the Royal Pagoda. Soldiers planned the conquest of the Moor and the downfall of the Turk in striped arbours surmounted by plumes of ostrich feathers. Admirals strode up and down the narrow pathways, glass in hand, sweeping the horizon and telling stories of the north-west passage and the Spanish Armada. Lovers dallied upon divans spread with sables. Frozen roses fell in showers when the Queen and her ladies walked abroad. Coloured balloons hovered motionless in the air. Here and there burnt vast bonfires of cedar and oak wood, lavishly salted, so that the flames were of green, orange, and purple fire. But however fiercely they burnt, the heat was not enough to melt the ice which, though of singular transparency, was yet of the hardness of steel. So clear indeed was it that there could be seen, congealed at a depth of several feet, here a porpoise, there a flounder. Shoals of eels lay motionless in a trance, but whether their state was one of death or merely of suspended animation which the warmth would revive puzzled the philosophers. Near London Bridge, where the river had frozen to a depth of some twenty fathoms, a wrecked wherry boat was plainly visible, lying on the bed of the river where it had sunk last autumn, over-laden with apples. The old bumboat woman, who was carrying her fruit to market on the Surrey side, sat there in her plaids and farthingales with her lap full of apples, for all the world as if she were about to serve a customer, though a certain blueness about the lips hinted the truth. 'Twas a sight King James specially liked to look upon, and he would bring a troupe of courtiers to gaze with him. In short, nothing could exceed the brilliancy and gaiety of the scene by day. But it was at night that the carnival was at its merriest. For the frost continued unbroken; the nights were of perfect stillness; the moon and stars blazed with the hard fixity of diamonds, and to the fine music of flute and trum-pet the courtiers danced.

*Virginia Woolf,* Orlando, *1928*

Christmas now packed away, one solitary decoration remains on the tree outside my house. Resting on a leafless elder branch just above the moonlit stream is a green and golden globe. I watch in wonder at my torchlight discovery, just a few metres from my back door, and am mesmerised by its beauty. Far more exquisite than any festive bauble, this feathered ball is a kingfisher, curled up to sleep through the windy January night. Sheltered on three sides by the arch of a stone road bridge, warming house wall and thorny briars of dog rose and bramble, this roost site is its secret winter refuge. Concealed deep in the shadows of the riverbank, the kingfisher sleeps undisturbed by the glare and noise as car headlights stream in a steady flow across the bridge above.

Buffeted by the winds, my avian high-wire artist continually rebalances – and, momentarily uncovering his all-black beak, I can see he is male, as female kingfishers have a reddish base to their lower mandible. Replacing his head under his wing into the fluffed feathered down, he returns to sleep. Illuminated by the torch I take one photo and then reluctantly shift the beam away to avoid disturbing him. Back in the house, my brief search online reveals no other photos of European kingfishers asleep – for such a well-photographed bird, this aspect of their lives is rarely witnessed. At dawn, when I look again, the branch is bare.

Kingfishers are known as ice birds in some countries, due to their seasonal migration away from cold weather. Harsh

winters are the ice birds' greatest enemy. Unable to fish effectively in frozen or swollen water, they are forced to leave their
freshwater territory and move to the coast, to its milder air and
unfrozen estuaries.

With their river high and flowing fast, my local pair have a
survival secret, a short distance upstream in the slow flowing
waters at Nind. Formerly a trout farm, but long since closed,
Nind's diverted stream and network of narrow pools and channels have returned to the wild. Cared for by Gloucestershire
Wildlife Trust, the original aim of the nature reserve's rebirth was
to extend the range of the nearby water vole population – locally
thriving, but nationally vulnerable. Successful for voles, and also
the hunting ground of water shrew, dipper and otter, Nind's tiny
wetland paradise is a favoured spot for the kingfishers, who in mid
winter must take advantage of every moment of daylight to feed.

Concealed in a tiny canvas hide at the end of a channel, I
watch as the male plunges into the pool – each flash of brilliance
so striking against a glistening scene of frost and sometimes
snow-laden vegetation. My stints in the hide are interspersed
with the appearance of other birds, a motionless heron or
water rail skulking through the withered reeds. Emerging
almost every second dive with fish, frustratingly for me this
king of fishers takes its prize to low hidden perches at the base
of the alder to dispatch and consume.

Despite their flamboyant feathers, kingfishers are surprisingly adept at camouflage, their rusty orange chest blending
well with bare wood. In daylight, or in the half light of dusk or
dawn, the blue behind their plumage appears as azure, cobalt
or steel, whereas the artificial lights of the flash of a camera at
night, show these as emerald, jade, sea green and even teal.

With the afternoon light fading and my cold endurance reached, I leave the hide and head home, following the kingfisher's journey downstream to our nocturnal roosts. Many birds have favoured roost sites that they return to each night so I'm hoping the kingfisher is a creature of habit!

Leaving Nind, the river winds around the edge of two fields, a well-walked footpath clinging to its bank for much of the route. In spring and summer these banks are a water-vole watcher's dream, where I while away many hours watching them feed on the celandine-covered banks and swimming in the clear water. Occasionally I'm treated to glimpses of voles in winter, when spells of milder weather bring them above ground, but today, as I crunch along the icy footpath home, this doesn't happen.

Reaching the village and revealing its industrial history, the river splits, one part diverted into a millstream. Channelled swiftly by high-sided stone walls through buildings, away from sight or foot access, the stream naturalises again by the old woollen mill and car repair garage. Crossing the road bridge, I'm distracted by gorgeous birdsong from the river below, not the shrill peeping of kingfisher in flight, but the melodious and bubbling notes of a territorial male dipper singing from a rock protruding in the dark water. Chocolate, chestnut and cream-coloured plumage, it's a challenge to spot the dipper in the dappled dusk stream. One of the earliest birds to breed, this dipper pair will very soon start to nest on an iron ledge under the mill.

Finally home, I'm anxious to see if the kingfisher returns again to his nocturnal perch. Timed to perfection, he arrives on the branch just as the final hint of daylight disappears. And saving its worst until last, the winter unleashes a long spell of snow. Framed by the arch of the road bridge, he endures freezing temperatures and blizzard conditions. The insulation of his four-season plumage is so good that the flurry of flakes settling on his feathers don't melt.

For a month the kingfisher slept through the dark hours of winter outside my house, just metres from back door. I took every opportunity to study him – even when it snowed at 2.30 a.m. I was there, standing knee deep in the river, in the darkness and covered in snow. Taking care to avoid disturbance, I always limited my photography to just a couple of shots each night.

And then, when mid February offered the first kiss of spring, my real-life sleeping beauty spent his final night asleep on that leafless elder branch. For him it's the time to think of pairing and nesting; for me it's the end of an enchanting month.

*Iain Green, 2016*

Incubus or Nightmare, though it commonly comes of a loaded stomach, will nevertheless often occur on the occasion of a change of weather in the night, which seem to produce the effect by disturbing the digestive organs. The same observation holds good with regard to those frightful and impressive dreams which some persons have in particular kinds of weather, and about the period of change. An east wind beginning to blow in the night will often cause them; and sometimes the same effect is produced by that state of the atmosphere which immediately precedes a large fall of snow; though the latter phenomenon more often produces dullness and languor of the whole animal system of the body.

Snow.—The indications of this phenomenon are pretty much the same as those of rain, and we must judge of its coming by the state of the thermometer, the time of year, and the wind then blowing. Many persons are unwell before large falls of snow.

*Thomas Furly Forster,* The Pocket Encyclopaedia of Natural Phenomena, *published 1827*

My brother John and I often roamed the snowy, rocky peaks of the Scottish mountains, but one walk in particular is etched in my memory. We had set off early, just before dawn, the sky a pink glow. The bitter chill of polar air made us flinch, and the coldness seeped, quickly and insidiously, into our boots, curling round our limbs and nipping our lungs.

In front of us the mountain path was frozen solid. A sheet of compacted, translucent ice had created a skating rink, weaving snake-like through jagged toothy crags. Far above hovered the summit of Beinn a'Chroin, a Munro south of Crianlarich. Smothered in dense cloud, its unilluminated bulky peak contrasted with the silver sky and snowfields, thick with pristine layers of new snow over old snow.

It was too cold to hang about, but we paused for a moment, letting our eyes follow the path until it disappeared round a turret of ice-capped crags. This was our final challenge of the day. We had already clambered to the summit of An Caisteal. Descending the col, to the lower slopes of Beinn a'Chroin, we had shuffled downhill on our bottoms when the path became treacherous.

All around us, undulating and conical peaks rose like slumbering giants, enduring winter with muted stoicism. The Alpenglow, when it came, was brief. For a few minutes, a reddish tinge heralded sunrise and the glens were swathed in its light, reminding me of a peacock's fanned tail, opalescent and regal, revealing a landscape of snow-dusted hills and sloping valleys sprinkled with rainbow-droplets of frozen cloud.

But winter was having none of it. This was not to be a day of sunshine and brightness. The early morning colours were swiftly chased away by freezing nebulae of mist that drifted down the hillsides. Daybreak's moment of glory faded, and a stubborn haze obscured our view of far-off treasures like Beinn Chabhair and Ben Nevis. We trudged by crystalline crags, clefts and ridges, hardly noticing distinctive features like Sron Gharbh and Twistin Hill. The sky was a mirage of shapeless, ashen cloud. There was nothing to see except vast expanses of stark whitewash. Mountain and sky merged to become an impenetrable palette.

As we stood at the edge of the path, I sensed a change in the weather. The morose terrain of Beinn a'Chroin encouraged the wind, which shifted the mist in ghostly strips. Bad weather was closing in. Easy to distinguish from other hills, the kenspeckle mass of the mountain was a place of winter only, an environment spectacularly bleak, beautiful and haunted.

I was spellbound. There are varying translations from Gaelic for Beinn a'Chroin, one being 'the Hill of Danger', but I preferred the more romantic 'Hill of the Cloven Foot'. The quietness and character of the mountain were enchanting. Common sense told me grass and heather must lurk below my boots, hidden away, awaiting the stirring of springtime, but it was impossible that day to imagine anything other than snow and ice. Winter was intransigent. It grasped the Munro in its hand, and would not loosen its grip. This was a land of eternal gloom and shadow, not an emerald city of shimmering peaks.

What captured me more than the vision of everlasting snowdrifts was the silence, rugged, still, hanging frozen in anticipation of the tempests to come. Our arctic tundra was soundless. No creature disturbed the tranquillity. There were no animal tracks to be seen. My hopes of spotting red deer, ptarmigans or mountain hares were dashed. We met no one else, but had the mountains to ourselves. I could have stood there all day but John, a Munro-bagger, was keen to press on.

Stepping onto the path, the click-click of our crampons echoed through the stillness. The neighbouring, wind-ruffled sastruga responded, as though saying 'hush, hush'. In retaliation for our intrusion, the wind picked up, slinking through the crags, singing its melancholy coronach and sounding like the woeful skirl of bagpipes. The weather blasted us with ferocious, horizontal blizzards of sleet and snow. This was winter at its purest, at its most dramatic. The sheer rawness enveloped me. I let big, fluffy snowflakes dissolve on my tongue. Heads bowed, we stumbled through the storms, undeterred by the hostility of the corries and palls of snow and mist. Beneath my snow-packed gloves my hands were numb and swollen.

In those moments when the snow abated, I snatched glimpses of the icy rock and lochan formations. This was not a day for admiring views or rubbing gritty fragments of moss and lichen between fingertips, yet there was something inspiring and invigorating about the Beinn's wintry spirit. It filled us with a sense of adventure and survival.

In the all-too-short periods of calm, I peeked through the gap in my hood, scanning the world around me. I was fearless in those days, but my stomach lurched at the steepness of the right-hand-sided gullies, where ice-clad shadows awaited any unfortunate victims unlucky enough to plummet into their midst.

At one point the path was blocked by crags. Instead of traversing the ridge to regain the track, we decided to climb a glacial crag, coated in a rock-hard waterfall. John went first. The bell-like chipping of his ice axe echoed over boulder and buttress. He made it look easy. Before long, he glanced down at me, grinning. My arm and leg muscles screamed, and my axe hardly made a dent in the ice. I struggled to find John's hand- and footholds, eventually managing to haul myself over the top and land in a heap, undignified but relieved.

I stood up to compose myself and just at that moment a sharp whistle pierced the silence. *Per, r, r, r, rit.* I managed to yank the hood from my face and glanced up in time to see a flock of eight sparrow-sized songbirds flicker by, tumbling down and skimming the ground before vanishing over a high, furrowed rock. Winter had kindly handed me something more exciting than deer or ptarmigans: snow buntings! With the birds' shrill twittering still ringing in our ears, we reached the summit in white-out conditions, and almost immediately headed northwards to join the descent path. The silence and the snow buntings were the highlights of the day, but winter had one more surprise for us. The snowfall ceased and the dusk sky became decorated with brushstrokes of twilight grey. The setting sun spread mandarin-tinted streaks, transforming the refrigerated moorland into a sea of twinkling stars, and glinting on the full-spate River Falloch. Weary, we dragged our way through the glen but my soul bristled with the lingering sounds and smells of Beinn a'Chroin.

I still carry that long-ago day deep, deep within. The memory of it is so vivid I can see the snow-coated peaks as clearly as I did then. I can hear my brother's voice and see his smile, and feel winter's icy chill flow through my veins. It is my most memorable winter, my most poignant. It was John's last winter.

*Jacqueline Bain, 2016*

My dear Mrs. Beecroft,

There are animals that sleep all the winter; – I am, I believe, become one of them: *they* creep into holes during the same season; – *I* have confined myself to the fireside of a snug parlour. If, indeed, a warm sunshiny day occurs, *they* sometimes creep out of their holes; – so, now and then, have *I*. *They* exist in a state of torpor; – so have *I* done: the only difference being, that *I* have all the while continued the habit of eating and drinking, which, to their advantage, *they* can dispense with. But my *mind* has certainly been asleep all the while; and whenever I have attempted to employ it, I have felt an oppression in my head which has obliged me to desist.

Stoke Newington, Jan. 1814

*Anna Laetitia Barbauld, 1814*

113

Two hundred jackdaws drape the skeleton of the winter beech like jet beads around the neck of a Victorian mourner. Gathering in the thin light of late afternoon the setting sun drags what's left of the day down into the valley. This hilltop tree isn't the jackdaws' final destination. Their calls are hard and feel cold on my skin as I stand half a mile to the east on a hill of my own.

Descending into the valley my steps reveal a grass-covered reservoir of sound-drowning water that drags the cries of the birds into a boggy silence beneath my feet. The noiselessness is disconcerting and I look up to check the jackdaws haven't flown, but their polished coal outlines are still there, etched into the sunset.

As I start to climb towards them I'm pelted by a hail of raucous caws. They're no longer a mass of birds; their behaviour shapes them into individual families, some numbering eight or nine, others just three or four. Silver-eyed adults oversee this year's milky blue-eyed young. Siblings jostle for position on the branches and within the family pecking-order. Fights seem commonplace; the loser sits alone, banished from the gregarious chattering like a sulky child on a naughty step.

Five summers ago a fledgling jackdaw appeared in our garden. Bald headed, except for a central strip of unruly feathers, its chimney-nesting parents ignored its constant cries for food. For the first few days it flapped up into the old apple tree at night and begged for food at the back door each morning, but with the progression of summer it learnt to fly. We watched in awe as it flung itself again and again from the roof of our house, crash landing in a pile of feathers and legs. Sometimes it stood quietly on my lap and delicately picked suet pellets from my hand, cocking its puzzled head this way and that as I talked. Then, one day, it flew away. We never saw it again.

The jackdaws' and rooks' ancient winter roost lies in a sheltered grove of tall trees nestling in the comfortable lap of a patchwork mire. On midwinter nights, when the cold drives most warm-blooded creatures together for warmth, this grove protectively hugs ten thousand birds.

Without warning the branches above me explode into a dark fabric of beating wings, raking the tree top with flailing claws. The jackdaws circle once, then head with a Flamenco flourish towards their roost. It's amazing how quickly the sound fades. The beech tree sighs and shivers as if a malevolent worry has been lifted from its shoulders, and a song thrush hesitantly tests out its repeated verses in the unexpected silence.

To watch the jackdaws' progress I half-run, half-walk to the rheumy grandmother of an oak that overlooks the valley. I run my fingers over her reassuringly knobbly bark and sit with my back against her moss-covered velvet trunk.

From every direction jackdaws and rooks, like wonky wheel spokes, radiate towards the roost half a mile below. Family groups stay close to each other within the confusion of weary wings, the promise of sleep and protection pulling them into the hub. I hear a strange sound. Several thousand birds fly directly over me, silent voiced; their soft black wings whooshing like a passenger train passing through a station.

Light fades further. Huge groups meet, join, lift and fall as the giant lung of jackdaws and rooks takes ever slower breaths.

Some tentatively land in the trees, but when a ripple of fear travels through the group they pour their liquid wings back into the sky. They circle as one agitated flock, the edges tatty with aging stragglers, the young jockeying for prime position near the front.

Sweeping in a shallow arc across the purple clouded sky an uneasy calm slowly returns. Reaching the roost small groups descend, falling like black, frozen hail; one minute in the air, the next gone, morphed into the shape of trees that expand, pregnant with soon-to-be sleeping birds.

Within the mass of settling corvids their individual voices are replaced by a wall of jumbled noise. Eventually, as the last few squeeze onto overloaded bunks, the dormitory lights extinguish and a blanket of quiet descends.

Stiff-legged I head back along the now moonlit path, scolded by greenfinches and sparrows whose gorse-protected slumber I have disturbed. A tawny owl calls to its mate; from across the valley she sends her come-get-me reply.

Halfway home sound explodes once more from the roost. In the dark, and without turning, I wait for the unseen but sensed danger to pass. Then, like the flick of a switch the sound stops – and silence, an enveloping silence, fills the valley until dawn.

*Jane Adams, 2016*

## Snowfall at Kernick

Here with a burly flutter and sting
 The snow-blast scampers winnowing,
And dribble of foam-flakes seeps and bores
 Through clay-clump thickets, under doors;
While flurry of snow-mist rises where
 The waggons tug till rails are bare.
The smoke is battered round the stacks;
 Soot falls with snow on trolley-tracks.
Even the mica-channel planks
 And narrow walls of settling-tanks
Are frilled and ice-splashed there between
 The frozen pools now sickly green.
The pit-edge merges with the fields,
 A softened gash the clay-bone shields;
Beyond it in the valley's fold
 Virginia woods loom taut and cold.

*Jack Clemo, 1961*

My feet are already chilled. The cold from the stone patio throbs through my heels, making my bones shake. Clumsily, numbly, I step onto the grass, where frozen spears seem to rake through my skin. I clench my toes. I've felt this before. Often, actually. But no matter how many times I return with feet so cold I imagine they, too, may turn to stone, I never seem to put shoes on. There is something wonderfully raw about going barefoot outside. And my body can't handle much else extreme.

It's not far to my destination, just a few metres to the low-slung chair that sits next to the left border of the lawn, sheltered by the still-brown leaves that cling to the beech hedge. Apart from my feet I am well wrapped up. I have to be.

They soon return. They've become used to my presence, over time. The robin in the bare forsythia never stopped singing. A mixed flock of finches (greenfinch and chaffinch, mostly) swoops over the garden, as they do on most days, to decimate the contents of the feeders, leaving behind only a cloud of seed husks. A great tit and a dunnock flit down to sit on top of the fence; the dunnock cocks its head, its dark red iris ablaze, watching. Goldfinches join the party. In winter they stick together.

I narrow my eyes and tilt back my head. I'm screened from the sheet of grey cloud that fills the sky by the tangle of branches above me. Like threaded brush strokes on a blank canvas, they'll soon be tipped with new buds, bristling with the promise of more. I sigh, then wince. It's not spring yet; in winter the air is so crisp it seems to scrape my lungs clean.

On the lawn, three parading town pigeons signal my urban location. They're accompanied by their more handsome cousins, the gentlemanly wood pigeons, one of whom wobbles over to the bird bath. It flops into the water, its feathers spilling out in all directions, splashing out almost every drop. For such an aristocratic-looking bird it seems a bit of a comedown.

The bird bath wasn't frozen this morning. Occasionally the ice has been so thick you could lift it out in one piece to examine its patterns, the water beginning to pool where gloved fingers hold it; put it on the grass and by midday it's gone. But this winter feels too mild. Today aside, we've only had two frosts.

We used to get snow at this time of year: I remember padding down to the hedge at the bottom of the garden, to curl beneath the leylandii and look up at the sky. Then snowflakes swarmed like mayflies and the ground was soft as sugar cake. Foxes made strange trails as they jumped through the snowdrifts and I imagined the mice tunnelling below. But not this winter. A part of the natural variation in climate, perhaps, but I fear the impact of climate change. The effects of it could destroy the faces of the seasons as we know them, upsetting the careful balance by which all living things flourish and fall. That aside, surely the way we now use our planet is wrong. At twenty-two I feel heavy with the weight of what the future could bring.

Too quickly my eyes grow fuzzy and I have to shut them a while. I can no longer rely on any one sense for too long. This is when my hearing takes over. Slowly, at first, I become aware of the clearer sounds around me – the harsh bark of a dog fox easily marked – but, gradually, as I listen more and more, I become attuned to the softer nuances of the dusk – the call of a blackbird, the thrum of a blue tit's wings, even the skulking rustle of a wren in the leaf litter behind me. This is nature's full score – evocative, unpredictable, inimitable. After years of neglecting to listen it feels as if I'm uncovering a secret world. The sounds, the smells, the *feel* of life is as much a part of the experience for me now.

I've been ill for four years. This will be my fifth. There are days when the reality of it beats down so heavily it feels like a winter's storm from which there seems no end. There are times so bleak I feel I'll never go on. It is during those moments I come outside. Here I sit a while, watching the mixed flocks gather, feeling the pigeons beat the air with their wings, hearing the robin sing. In nature, in solitude, I find an inner strength. I let this place take up the weight of my burdens: it will hold them in the boughs of the swaying beech, in the threads of the evening chorus, in the vastness of the iron sky. When I go inside, my load seems a little lighter.

There are moments of peace even in the darkest of times. When life is stripped to its purest core we find its resolve is strong. And when the world around me is so cold it nearly takes my breath away, when my feet feel they might just be snatched from beneath me, I will push on – on to the grass, towards the other side, and to my destination: to sit, and rest there a while, until time and nature have thawed my heart and fears.

*Elizabeth Guntrip, 2016*

In some winters there is a rush of waxwings to Britain; their presence in numbers is then reported from many parts of the country. A few years ago a flock of about thirty spent two or three days round the ponds at Fallodon. I was unfortunately away from home, but a friend saw and watched them. They were feeding apparently on the red berries of viburnum (water elder), which seem not to be a favourite food of our resident birds, for they are left on the bushes till quite late in the year. Mountain-ash berries, on the other hand, are taken as soon as they are ripe; especially by mistle-thrushes, whose harsh chuckle about a mountain-ash tree is one of the common sounds of early autumn. The waxwing, I suppose, gets its name from some peculiar bright red feathers that look like drops of sealing-wax on the wing. Waxwing is at any rate a shorter and more pleasing name than 'Bohemian chatterer', which is the alternative.

Another winter bird, still more rare, I have seen only once. It was on a January afternoon, a Sunday; I was walking along a plain public road on my way to post letters: there being no postman on Sunday, we often had to do this, and it was looked upon as a somewhat humdrum business, for the post-office was three miles away and the road commonplace. Suddenly my attention was aroused by the note of a blackbird; it was more than the ordinary alarm note which blackbirds give when disturbed: it was a note that suggested terror. The blackbird flew along the hedge and sought cover therein; after it came a bird of about the same size, with smooth flight and a rather long tail: this second bird lit in a small bare hedgerow tree in front of me, and gave me a clear and satisfactory view of a great grey shrike. It did not appear to me that the shrike was actually in pursuit of or seriously threatening the blackbird, and the terror of the latter at the mere appearance of the shrike was remarkable. A year or two later, when I was in London and could not get home, it was reported to me early in March that a great grey shrike was seen for some days in a plantation near the house. It frequented a spot where long-tailed tits were used to build every spring. One of these tits was found slaughtered while the shrike was about the place, and there was no long-tailed tit's nest in this plantation that year.

*Sir Edward Grey,* The Charm of Birds, *1927*

The otters were alarmed by the coming of the man, and that night they left the headland, returning to the Burrows, and hunting rabbits in the great warren of the sandhills. A cold mist lay on the plains and in the hollows, riming the marram grasses and the withered stems of thistle and mullein, so that in the morning mildew and fungi in strange plant forms seemed to have grown out of the sand. On the coarser hairs of the otters' coats the hoar remained white, but on the shorter and softer hairs it melted into little balls of water. Everything except the otters and birds and bullocks was white. The sedges and reeds of the duckponds were white, so was the rigging of the ketches in the pill. The hoofholes of cattle were filmed with brittle ice. In the cold windless air came distinct the quacking of ducks and the whistling of drakes as the wildfowl flighted from the ponds and saltings to the sea, where they slept by day.

The otters lay up near a cattle shippen, among reeds with white feathery tops. A dull red sun, without heat or rays, moved over them, sinking slowly down the sky. For two days and two nights the frosty vapour lay over the Burrows, and then came a north wind which poured like liquid glass from Exmoor and made all things distinct. The wind made whips of the dwarf willows, and hissed through clumps of great sea-rushes. The spines of the marram grasses scratched wildly at the rushing air, which passed over the hollows where larks and linnets crouched with puffed feathers. Like a spirit freed by the sun's ruin and levelling all things before a new creation the wind drove grains of sand against the legs and ruffled feathers of the little birds, as though it would breathe annihilation upon them, strip their frail bones of skin and flesh, and grind them until they become again that which was before the earth's old travail. Vainly the sharp and hard points of the marram grasses drew their circles on the sand: the Icicle Spirit was coming, and no terrestrial power could exorcise it.

The north wind carried a strange thickset bird which drifted without feather sound over the dry bracken of Ferny Hill, where Tarka and Greymuzzle had gone for warmth. Its plumage was white barred and spotted with dark brown. Its fierce eyes were ringed with yellow, the colour of the lichens on the stone shippens. Mile after mile its soft and silent wings had carried it, from a frozen land where the Northern Lights stared in stark perpetuity upon the ice-fields. The thickset bird was an Arctic Owl, and its name was Bubu, which means Terrible. It quartered the mires and the Burrows, and the gripe of its feathered feet was death to many ducks and rabbits.

Clouds moved over the land and sea with the heavy grey drifting silence of the ice-owl's flight; night came starless, loud with the wind's rue in the telegraph wires on the sea-wall. As Tarka and his mate were running down to meet the flood-tide in the pill, a baying broke out in the sky; whiskered heads lifted fixed to harken. For a minute the otters did not move, while the hound-like baying passed over. The long skein of south-wending geese swung round into the wind, flying with slow flaps and forming a chevron that glided on down-held, hollow wings beyond the pill-mouth. Cries of golden plover, twined in the liquid bubble-link of the curlews' chain-songs, rose up from the saltings.

The white-fronted geese, eaters of grass and clover, had come before the blizzard howling its way from the North Star. A fine powdery snow whirled out of the sky at night, that lay nowhere, but raced over the mossy plains and hillocks, and in the Burrows, faster than the grains of sand. Tree, dune, shippen, and dyke – all were hid in whirling white chaos at daylight. The next day thicker snowflakes fell, and out of the storm dropped a bird with white wings, immensely swift in flight, whose talon-stroke knocked off the head of a goose. It stood on the slain, holding by the black sickle-claws of its yellow feet; its hooked beak tore breast-bone and flesh together. Its plumage was brown-spotted like the plumage of Bubu – the hue of snow and fog. Every feather was taut and cut for the swiftest stoop in the thin airs of its polar ranging. Its full brown eyes glanced proudly as any Chakchek, for it was a Greenland falcon.

Beyond the shaped and ever-shifting heaps of sand, beyond the ragged horizon of the purple-grey sea, the sun sunk as though it were spent in space, a dwarfed star quenching in its own steam of decay. The snow fled in the wind, over the empty shells of snails and rabbit skeletons lying bare and scattered, past the white, sand-stripped branches of dead elderberry trees, and the dust of them aided an older dust to wear away the living tissue of the Burrows. Night was like day, for neither moon nor sun nor star was seen. Then the blizzard passed, and the snow lay in its still pallor under the sky.

*Henry Williamson,* Tarka the Otter, *1927*

Hickling Broad nature reserve hides a dark secret. A dark but wonderful secret that only visitors who come in deepest winter and stay for that magical hour, '*l'heure contre chien et loup*', experience. It is then, as the sun westers, dipping below clouds and for a precious few minutes lights and transforms Hickling's reeds with a warm fiery glow, that a gathering takes place. A silent coming-together from many directions of powerful wings, keen eyes and strong, hooked beaks. A coming-together under the falling cloak of night of one of the great congregations of rare birds of prey in England.

You don't have to visit Hickling at twilight, of course. The wild, windswept, reedy marshland of this nature reserve is beautiful at any time of year and any time of day. In winter, Hickling's silver-headed reeds sway and dance to the music of cold winds. Should your visit be blessed with early morning sunshine, almost every silver reed 'feather' is wreathed with dewy spider silk. This early morning magic vanishes by mid morning, except on misty days, when the mist itself coats each reed with jewels of dew.

In spring and summer this reserve is busy with life; swallowtails dance over brightly coloured marsh flowers while a whole symphony of warblers – reed, sedge and Cetti's – serenade visitors from the hidden depths of summer-green reeds. So why on earth visit in midwinter, when, in contrast, Hickling so often seems devoid of life?

For me the silent winter landscape of this wild place holds

a special magic, echoing powerfully with feelings deep inside me. Like strong winds and storms Hickling's winter silence puts me in touch with an inner wildness. It makes me feel part of this place, more connected somehow than when I walk here in summer. It's funny how silence is sometimes so much louder, or deeper, than words. And of course there is wildlife to find, though when the cold bites, and winter winds blow, wildlife hunkers down, finding hidden sheltered spots which lie largely out of sight.

My walk along the boardwalks and reserve paths this January afternoon is quiet, but punctuated by sudden explosions of life. A coot patters across open water then vanishes into reeds; a hidden snipe startles into flight out of nowhere; a flock of lapwings, black and white against the sky, twinkle overhead then disappear into the distance; a kestrel appears hovering motionless against the wind then glides out of sight; a hidden jay gives a single raucous scream, only deepening the silence. Nature is here, but much of the time wind, sky and reed seem empty. However, I've been told that at sunset on these short, cold days a gathering of rare and magnificent wildlife may happen; that Hickling may reveal its dark secret.

As with most such spectacles timing is everything. You need to know both where and when to go. And in this case the where is a viewpoint, just a short walk away, adjacent to a landmark, the ancient brick tower of Stubb Mill. The when is deepest winter. And the time is just before sunset.

I arrive a good hour before. The sun is low and, though it's only mid afternoon, with a clear sky overhead the temperature is already falling. My view from a low bank next to the old Broads drainage mill sweeps across a wild flat panorama of marshland, a landscape tapestry woven in marsh browns and sedge greys. I can see all the way to the coast. In the distance the wind turbines of Winterton are clearly visible, and, much closer, the evocative and distinctive outline of another Broads drainage mill, Brograve, the ruins of which stand stark, skeletal and lonely. Surrounded by marsh its ruined sails give testament to changing times and vanished ways of life. It doesn't take much to imagine the coastal dunes of Horsey and Winterton being breached in a winter storm and the tide sweeping across this low, watery land where nothing seems to stand between you and the distant sea.

The way to discover Hickling's secret is to wait. Like so many wildlife secrets it will be revealed only to the patient. But waiting here has its rewards. Not just one barn owl but three hover and hunt over the marsh. Who could ever tire of watching barn owls? They seem to float weightlessly over dyke, marsh and reeds, before plunge-diving on folded wings into clumps of sedge and rush, vanishing in pursuit of hapless voles. I'm lucky, as yet another owl appears, quartering the marsh. This one, though equally buoyant in flight, has longer and narrower wings, browner plumage and distinctive staring yellow eyes. This short-eared owl is a winter visitor here but seems happy to hunt alongside its resident paler cousins.

Despite wrapping up warmly, the cold is beginning to bite. But I don't have to wait long for the first stars of this show to put in their appearance. It's still an hour or so before sunset when the marsh harriers appear drifting silently on spread wings across the marsh in the mid distance – first in ones and twos, then as many as a dozen cavort in the air at once. My count by sunset is forty-five but more than seventy of these magnificent birds are sometimes seen here. Incredible to think that back in the early 1970s only one or two pairs were found in the whole of Britain.

Marsh harriers are not the only stars this evening. In the distance a thinner-winged, lighter brown harrier appears with a distinctive white rump. My first hen harrier this year. This is closely followed by a silver-grey male, his smaller size and elegant black wing tips making the larger marsh harriers look almost ungainly. Hen harriers are Britain's most persecuted bird of prey, at least on their northern breeding grounds. It's good to know these two have chosen a nature reserve for their night-time roost. To see so many harriers in one place, and two species, is truly amazing – but the best is yet to come. Arriving almost in the dark, a grand finale announced by distant bugling calls, nine common cranes pass overhead, flying into the gathering dark with outstretched necks and trailing legs. These cranes, rarest avian stars of the Norfolk Broads, silhouetted against a night sky and lit only by the faint, pink afterglow of the setting sun, pass over my head in moments. But this memory of one of Norfolk's great winter wildlife spectacles will last a lifetime.

*David North, 2016*

The air of the room chilled his shoulders. He stretched himself cautiously along under the sheets and lay down beside his wife. One by one they were all becoming shades. Better pass boldly into that other world, in the full glory of some passion, than fade and wither dismally with age. He thought of how she who lay beside him had locked in her heart for so many years that image of her lover's eyes when he had told her that he did not wish to live.

Generous tears filled Gabriel's eyes. He had never felt like that himself towards any woman, but he knew that such a feeling must be love. The tears gathered more thickly in his eyes and in the partial darkness he imagined he saw the form of a young man standing under a dripping tree. Other forms were near. His soul had approached that region where dwell the vast hosts of the dead. He was conscious of, but could not apprehend, their wayward and flickering existence. His own identity was fading out into a grey impalpable world: the solid world itself which these dead had one time reared and lived in was dissolving and dwindling.

A few light taps upon the pane made him turn to the window. It had begun to snow again. He watched sleepily the flakes, silver and dark, falling obliquely against the lamplight. The time had come for him to set out on his journey westward. Yes, the newspapers were right: snow was general all over Ireland. It was falling on every part of the dark central plain, on the treeless hills, falling softly upon the Bog of Allen and, farther westward, softly falling into the dark mutinous Shannon waves. It was falling, too, upon every part of the lonely churchyard on the hill where Michael Furey lay buried. It lay thickly drifted on the crooked crosses and headstones, on the spears of the little gate, on the barren thorns. His soul swooned slowly as he heard the snow falling faintly through the universe and faintly falling, like the descent of their last end, upon all the living and the dead.

*James Joyce,* Dubliners, *1914*

January and it's been raining for weeks. The Thames is just a day away from flooding when I head down to the old ferry crossing to Moulsford and take the towpath towards Little Stoke.

My walk begins more as an effort than a pleasure. Deep mud makes every step a squelch and a slip and a twist. Even my dog, Luka, isn't particularly happy. He high-trots like a dressage pony, slow enough not to slide, fast enough not to sink. For about half a mile, I see nothing but where to place my next foot.

But I am hearing things from every direction. And not tracing those sounds with vision lends a difference to this walk. The mud is incredibly close and in focus. Everything else retreats. It becomes not exactly distant, just present in a separate space. It's a strangely connecting dislocation. Like a child's belief in the invisibility conveyed by her fingers, or a prayer to an unknown god.

The rain has only recently stopped pouring. The birds sing a subdued winter song.

Strangely, there's no noise from the river. Nothing from the Greylags or the Canada geese. None of their usual honking contests or flight races under the bridge. In fact, everything watery is silent. A respectful muting at that. It's as if something is waiting to happen. But what?

I stop for a moment to re-focus. Yes, the river is still here but so hushed. I can feel an unseen mist hanging over the water, but sign of the mist there is not. Maybe it lifted moments before we got here and I sense it in the same way that you sense the presence of the dead just after death. Maybe not.

The goose island is actually empty. Not a single one of the gaggle remains. Just a holiday schoolyard silence. Odd.

I walk into the cavern of the railway bridge just as a train screams its way overhead. Luka hates it when that happens and he huddles into my leg. But for me the silence still isn't really broken. It's as if I've sidestepped out of time to a different place. I've not crossed between worlds, I don't mean that. I'm just in my own removed space.

It's a state slightly helped by the absence of other people, but solitude doesn't feel key. If someone came now, it seems that I would slide by without them noticing. They'd just sense the passing of a mist. Or get the feeling of someone watching them, and turn and look back to check. And then perhaps I'd re-materialise like a deer out of shadows in the woods.

Or maybe they'd be the invisible one and I'd be the one looking back. What I'm feeling doesn't feel personal. Anyone walking here might slip into the same mysterious place.

The footpath moves into open fields and I can walk beside it out of the mud. Luka's stride joyfully lengthens. The river keeps its snail's pace to our left. And, far off to the right, one field away's distance, the geese wait silently in the grass.

*Emma Kemp, 2016*

### *Lucy Gray, or Solitude*

*Oft I had heard of Lucy Gray:*
*And, when I crossed the wild,*
*I chanced to see, at break of day,*
*The solitary child.*

*No mate, no comrade Lucy knew;*
*She dwelt on a wide Moor –*
*The sweetest Thing that ever grew*
*Beside a human door!*

*You yet may spy the Fawn at play,*
*The Hare upon the green;*
*But the sweet face of Lucy Gray*
*Will never more be seen.*

*'To-night will be a stormy night –*
*You to the town must go;*
*And take the lantern, Child, to light*
*Your mother through the snow.'*

*'That, Father! will I gladly do;*
*'T is scarcely afternoon, –*
*The minster-clock has just struck two,*
*And yonder is the moon!'*

*At this the father raised his hook,*
*And snapp'd a fagot-band;*
*He plied his work; – and Lucy took*
*The lantern in her hand.*

*Not blither is the mountain roe:*
*With many a wanton stroke*
*Her feet disperse the powdery snow,*
*That rises up like smoke.*

*The storm came on before its time:*
*She wander'd up and down;*
*And many a hill did Lucy climb*
*But never reached the town.*

*The wretched parents all that night*
*Went shouting far and wide;*
*But there was neither sound nor sight*
*To serve them for a guide.*

*At day-break on the hill they stood*
*That overlooked the moor;*
*And thence they saw the bridge of wood,*
*A furlong from their door.*

*They wept, – and, turning homeward, cried,*
*'In heaven we all shall meet'; –*
*When in the snow the mother spied*
*The print of Lucy's feet.*

Then downwards from the steep hill's edge
They tracked the footmarks small;
And through the broken hawthorn-hedge,
And by the long stone-wall;

And then an open field they crossed:
The marks were still the same;
They tracked them on, nor ever lost,
And to the bridge they came.

They followed from the snowy bank
The footmarks, one by one,
Into the middle of the plank,
And further there were none!

– Yet some maintain that to this day
She is a living child;
That you may see sweet Lucy Gray
Upon the lonesome wild.

O'er rough and smooth she trips along,
And never looks behind;
And sings a solitary song
That whistles in the wind.

*William Wordsworth, 1799*

Late one January, three friends and I climbed Beinn a'Chaorainn, the Hill of the Rowan, near Loch Laggan in Scotland. The day began magnificently. Galleons of cloud were at full sail in the sky, racing slowly over the blueness. The sunshine was hard and bright, the snow tuning the light to its own white frequency. Despite the coldness of the air, or perhaps because of it, as the four of us walked into the mountain I could feel the blood pulsing warmly in my toes and fingers, and the sun burning on the edges of my cheeks.

From the roadside the Hill of the Rowan rises to three distinct tops. On its east flank, visible and forbidding, are two glacier-carved cirques which were gouged out of the mountain during the Pleistocene. That day the steep cliffs of the cirques were dense with ice, which flashed and glittered in the sunlight as we approached them. We passed first through a copse of pine trees, and then emerged on to open ground, where we crossed several wide swathes of sphagnum moss. In summer these would have been tremulous and brimming with rainfall, as wobbly as water-beds. But winter had hammered them into stasis and glazed them with ice. Looking down into the clear ice as I walked over it, I could see the moss, dense and colourful as a carpet, yellow-green stars of butterwort dotted here and there.

We began to ascend one of the east-facing ridges of the mountain, which separated the two icy cirques. As we climbed, the weather changed its mood. The clouds thickened and slowed in the sky. The light became unstable, flicking from silver to dirty grey. After an hour of climbing it began to snow heavily.

Approaching the top of the mountain, we were in near white-out conditions, and it was hard to separate the air and the land. It had become much colder. My gloves had frozen into rigid shells, which clunked hollowly when I knocked them together, and a thick scab of white ice had built up on my balaclava where my breath came through it, like a clumsy clown's mouth.

A few hundred yards from the summit the ridge flattened out, and we were able to unrope safely. The others stopped for something to eat, but I moved on ahead, wanting to enjoy the solitude of the white-out. The wind was blowing along the ridge towards me, and under its invisible pressure everything was on the move. Millions of particles of snow dust streamed just above the ground in a continuous flow. Rounded chunks of old hard snow were being blown reluctantly along, skidding over the surface of the ridge. And the big soft flakes which were falling from the sky were being driven into me by the wind. They walloped almost soundlessly against my clothing, and I built up a thin fur of snow on my windward side. It seemed as though I were wading upcurrent in a loose white river. I could see no more than five yards in any direction, and I felt utterly and excitingly alone. The world beyond the whirled snow became unimportant, almost unimaginable. I could have been the last person on the planet.

After several minutes' walking I reached the small summit plateau of the mountain and stopped. A few paces away, sitting and contemplating me, hunkered back on its huge hind legs, its tall ears twitching, was a snow hare. It seemed curious at this apparition on its mountain-top, but unalarmed. The hare was a clean white all over, except for its black tail, a small patch of grey on its chest and the two black rims of its ears. It moved on a few paces in its odd gait, its rear legs shunting its hindquarters slowly forward and up, almost over its head. Then it stopped again. For half a minute we stood there in the blowing snow, in the strange silence of the snowstorm. Me with my clown's mouth of ice, the hare with its lush white coat and polished black eyes.

And then my friends emerged like spectres from the whiteout, their climbers' hardware clanking. Immediately the hare kicked away with a spurt of snow, swerving and zigzagging off into the blizzard, delicately but urgently, its black tail bobbing long after its body had disappeared.

I stayed on the top of the mountain for a while and let the others walk on ahead to begin the descent. I thought about the snow hare; about how for an animal like this to cross one's path was to be reminded that it had a path too – that I had crossed the snow hare's path as much as it had crossed mine. Then my mind moved away from the mountain-top. The solitude I had experience in the white-out on the ridge had been replaced by a sense of the distance invisibly before me. I no longer felt cocooned by the falling snow, I felt accommodated by it, extended by it – part of the hundreds of miles of landscape over which the snow was falling. I thought east, to where the snow would be falling over the 1,000 million-year-old granite backs of the Cairngorm mountains. I thought north, to where snow would silently be covering the empty wilderness of the Monadhliaths, the Grey Hills. I thought west, to where snow would be falling on the great peaks of the Rough Bounds of Knoydart – Ladhar Bheinn, the Hill of the Claw; Meall Buidhe, the Yellow Hill; and Luinne Bheinn, the Hill of Anger. I thought of the snow falling across ridge on ridge of the invisible hills, and I thought too that there was nowhere at that moment I would rather be.

*Robert Macfarlane,* Mountains of the Mind, *2003*

Emerging from sleep I was aware of a far-off prolonged howling. Poking my head out from under the eiderdown I saw a white glow framed by the window and knew instantly what it signified. An amazing sight was waiting for me as I wiped away the condensation and peered out. Elmsleigh Road was a river of drifting snow and flakes like white tracer bullets sped from blackness into the street lights. Snow smoked and fumed and fretted, and I could see the treetops bending in Mr Mortimer's garden at the bottom of the terrace and feel the cold pushing through the glass into my nose which was pressed against the window. O God, I prayed, don't let it stop. Let it fall for a week and please make it settle. If I hadn't been shivering so much I wouldn't have gone back to bed but it was the warmest place and I was still drowsy despite the excitement.

Next morning there was a white light on the ceiling and outside random flakes fell from a grey sky into a white hush. Dad remained happily in bed and Mam cursed the weather both he and I loved for different reasons. When I ate my porridge she stared out at the drifts and sucked her breath through her teeth and said:

'The wind's coming off the sea again. There's more snow on the way. Damned horrible stuff. Damned winter.'

I grinned gleefully at Nibs. Mam preferred her snow in the Mabinogion or *Pickwick Papers* but snow in the town meant trouble and hard work.

'I can't get the back door open,' she grunted. Then she raised her voice so that Dad would hear.

'Perhaps Lord Muck will heave his carcass off the mattress before dinner time and give us a hand.'

'I'm asleep,' Dad said. 'Send for the council. Make those idle buggers earn their wages.'

I pulled on my wellingtons and buttoned my mac over my corduroy lumber jacket, and Mam straightened my balaclava.

'Don't you go far,' she said. 'And keep that scarf across your chest or you'll be coughing phlegm.'

I crammed the cheese and chutney sandwiches and three jam tarts in Dad's old fishing bag and cautiously opened the front door. The wind had risen again and was sculpting the drifts. I had never seen so much snow.

'Brian,' Mam called.

'I'm only going to Gran's,' I lied and ploughed up the terrace in case she changed her mind and decided to keep me in by the fire.

Beyond the deserted streets the savage north easterly was lifting the surface powder and whisking it away in white clouds and columns. A coppery glow lit the sky just above the sea and the sound of heavy surf carried inland to magnify the sense of desolation. Snow fell from the wind-scurry, lovely whiteness to cancel out civilisation; and mallard came low and untidy in the teeth of the blizzard, each flight unsure and noisy. But above the shriek of the wind I heard the music of high-flying geese and saw the dark lines of birds lifting and falling. A desire for some unravished, unknown place made me hold my breath and wish. A blast of snow sent me reeling. The marshes and water-meadows were alive with wildfowl and the double-clap of a twelve-bore filled the air with wings. Tacker was at work, visiting the traps he had set in the mud for ducks. He shot oystercatchers, curlew and herons that winter and left them lifeless for scavengers to pick clean. His path to hell was littered with murdered creatures. But two selves were warring in my own body – one the hunter who could gather a shot mallard from the reeds and see only the carcass glazed with honey lying in state among the roast potatoes, peas and carrots; the other, the novice priest who worshipped nature and ran on the high octane fuel of idealism and romance. Later I would experience a blinding moment of revelation on my personal Road to Damascus and never kill a creature again.

All day I wandered through the valley and the woods, seeking out the deepest drifts, skidding across the solid ponds and drainage guts. I was at the centre of a whining gloom and sometimes I felt curiously dazed and weightless, and thought the winter was trying to tell me something. Or maybe those pure animal men who had lived here before history had spoken the language of the wind and the trees, and had left the deathless part of themselves in the field corners and on the hilltops.

From such mysteries I plodded on to the agonising beauty of sunset and found a dead pigeon by Broome Linhay. It had been shot and had fallen beyond the nose of the sportsman's dog.

The sky cleared a little at dimpsey and revealed the moon in its last quarter. Rabbits pushed their way out of the blocked warrens and stared across the whiteness. Against the hedges the poor, miserable sheep steamed and bleated. They were always left out in rough weather but the cattle were brought indoors. I tried not to disturb them as I approached the potato clamp and excavated enough Red Soils for the Sunday meal. And quite suddenly I was tired and hungry. I had walked in a great circle past Cider Mill Farm, up over the fields to Windy Corner and back to Cider Mill Hill, New Road Forest and Broome Linhay. Between two reefs of cloud was the star-spangled way. Then it vanished and the wind cut as cruelly as it sang, and I walked the white road past the black houses under the black clouds. The front of my coat was a sheet of ice and my balaclava had frozen to my ears.

'Look at the state of you,' Mam cried. 'D'you think I've nothing better to do than wash your clothes? Get in by the fire and I'll heat some water for your bath.'

But she was glad to see me and recounted in detail the minutiae of her day. Thawing out at the fireside in vest and pants I listened to the end of Children's Hour and the crackle of frying kippers.

*Brian Carter,* Yesterday's Harvest, *1982*

In the west the winter sky is streaked with cirrus clouds that look as if they have been combed across the heavens by a giant hand. A weak sun filters through as it sinks towards the horizon, turning them a gentle peach. In the east the sky is clear, a cold cerulean blue fading to creamy white as it nears the earth. Any warmth there may have been in the faint sunshine rapidly vanishes as evening approaches and a deep chill settles in the air. I thrust my hands in my pockets and stamp my feet to ward off the cold. A noisy bunch of rooks fly overhead, checking out potential roosting sights. They abandon a nearby oak tree in favour of a distant wood and quiet settles over the sleeping landscape.

I set off briskly to my vantage point in the disused quarry workings where the River Ure used to flow. Now that the valuable gravel has been removed, the land has flooded and forms part of a nature reserve. I hadn't expected it to be this cold so early and am wondering about the wisdom of abandoning the fireside in order to pursue my quest. I keep stopping for a few moments to scan the sky with binoculars, but every time it is empty. At my destination I check again. Nothing. I start to doubt myself and wonder if I'm wasting my time. It's getting colder and the sun has just dropped out of sight.

And then, there they are. Only a few at first, flying just above the treetops in a group, tiny black specks against the sky. They fly from left to right and back left again, joining up with another, larger group. The combined force seems to act as if it were a magnet, drawing more and more birds into the throng. They seem to appear out of nowhere, birds coming from all directions. They keep coming, one group after another. Where have they been hiding all day? How come I haven't noticed them earlier? I wonder if they are celebrating meeting up again after a day's foraging, as they chase each other and share the day's news. Within twenty minutes, I estimate there must be about thirty thousand of them.

They move individually yet as one, swooping and diving with such grace and harmony it's like watching liquid pour across the sky. Sometimes they space themselves out, almost disappearing from view, then they re-form in a tight gathering. The fluid shapes of the flocks are always changing, drifting from one configuration to another, and then on to another in a never-ending dance. They flow like a shoal of fish in the currents of the ocean or perhaps as smoke rising from a bonfire.

A new leader periodically arises from within the cloud of birds and a group splits off, swoops away, turns around and re-joins the main flock. The birds then turn back on themselves forming a darker patch where there is a double layer of individuals. The dance continues as the cloud explodes and coalesces, creating ever-changing patterns. I have not seen a single bird out of place and there have been no mid-air collisions, so I can only conclude that they are following an invisible master choreographer.

Now they are flying over me. There are birds to my right, to my left, in front, behind and above me – hundreds of them. They are flying in complete silence, the only sound being that of all those feathered wings moving through the air. I hold my breath. The world stands still. Suddenly, I am no longer the observer of a spectacle but have been invited to become an integral part of it.

Continuing their aerial show, the birds fly on, twisting and twirling, weaving and wafting. The colours have now drained from the sky as dusk settles over us. I notice the birds are collecting in a tighter flock and quite suddenly a few hundred of them pour out of the sky like sugar grains flowing off a teaspoon. They have said their 'good nights' and are ready to roost in the reeds below. The remaining birds continue to fly in a cloud, spilling out a thousand or so, here and there, until they all reach their roost and the sky is empty once again.

I am cold – very cold. I can't feel my hands or feet. But it doesn't matter. I'll not forget this experience as long as I live. The spectacle has been mesmerising, awe-inspiring and humbling.

How is it that a load of starlings can move together with such accord in complete harmony and in such numbers? What music are they dancing to that humans no longer hear?

*Janet Willoner, 2016*

## The Gipsy Camp

*The snow falls deep; the Forest lies alone:*
*The boy goes hasty for his load of brakes,*
*Then thinks upon the fire and hurries back;*
*The Gipsy knocks his hands and tucks them up,*
*And seeks his squalid camp, half hid in snow,*
*Beneath the oak, which breaks away the wind,*
*And bushes close, with snow like hovel warm:*
*There stinking mutton roasts upon the coals,*
*And the half roasted dog squats close and rubs,*
*Then feels the heat too strong and goes aloof;*
*He watches well, but none a bit can spare,*
*And vainly waits the morsel thrown away:*
*'Tis thus they live – a picture to the place;*
*A quiet, pilfering, unprotected race.*

*John Clare, 1841*

One of the perks of being carter were choosing your own team of horses. Most carters 'ud go for youth and beauty, but I collared old Jolly and Prince because I'd worked with them before and knowed their even temperament. They warn't a matching pair; Jolly were a mahogany, and Prince – borned at Woodstock like his royal namesake – were the Black Prince. Jolly were seventeen hands and Prince were sixteen and a half. With Jolly in the furrow and Prince on the ridge, us was working all on the level.

First job as carter, lifting the latch of the stable all by myself at five o'clock of a dark winter's morn, be to light the stable lamp. It were a hurricane-lamp, hung on the beam, and I'd light it as I'd seen Joe Maycock light it, with one of they old brimstone lucifers, striking it one-handed across the rump of me ridge'n'furrowed corduroy breeches. Its soft swinging glow 'ud alight upon Jolly – Violet – Prince – Daisy – and come to rest over Bowler-the-Biter and others beyond, their rumps glimpsed glossy in their knowed stalls in the stable. They was all over sixteen hands: mostly the old Suffolk, with one or two Canadian Punch, and Boxer the heavyweight Shire.

I'd fill the sidlip, the large round shallow rush-basket we used to use when sowing seed by hand, and bait the horses, teasing the mixed corn and chaff thinly along the manger so's they licked rather than scoffed. Baiting stopped 'em bolting their food, made 'em give each mouthful thirty chews – good for 'em on an empty stomach. Good for *my* empty stomach too – gave I a bit o' peace to eat my breakfast without 'em all standing round, cadging.

There was four pairs, and Polly for the odd jobs, carting swedes to the sheep and churns to the station. I'd turn 'em out in pairs to drink at the trough in the yard while I swept the muck into a ready-yup for old Gramp, Bartholomew Chaundy, to do the farming-out. Then I'd put out a fuller feed. They'd saunter back of their own accord, knowing they was due for their main course.

While waiting for the men to turn up I'd start grooming my team and polishing their harness. Even when I had only old Bartholomew and a couple of bwoy-chaps as labour, us took a pride in our teams and harness, often turning up early or staying a bit late. You warn't paid for the extra time spent on spit'n'polish, you took a pride in being all ready and well-turned-out in the yard with your team by the time Mr Lennox came at seven to give the carter his orders.

'*Et!*' – it were a powerful moment for me, my first time as carter, giving the traditional Oxfordsheer carter's command for the teams to set forth. They talks of a pride of lions; us had a 'pride of Punches' (and mighty Boxer done us proud on the Shire). The true Suffolk Punch be always 'chesnut', spelled just as it were writ in 1768 when the first foal were recorded. There be seven shades of chesnut from Captain's 'bright golden' to Prince's 'deep brown-black', all still identifiable today as they was first classed in the 1877 stud-book.

The Canadian Punch be all colours; ours were grey. Some slave-driving farmers had only grey or light-coloured horses on their farms so they could spy from a distance if their men be still toiling, nose to the plough, traipsing across the landscape.

Mr Lennox warn't that harsh a taskmaster. After he'd gived the orders for the day he'd trust us to collect our tucker-bags, top-cwoats and nosebags from the pile by the trough and go and plod on with it. When I were short-handed he'd come and take a team hisself, working alongside. The farmer were often one on you in they days.

If we was going to plough afresh we'd have a fairish walk, driving the implement behind our team along the muddy road, down Fulwell, past 'lotment Hill and up on the hill to Henel Field; or, in the other direction, along the narrow Fulwell Lane up to the turnpike along the Charlbury Road to New Piece. If we was carrying on from the day before, our implements was already up in the field and we'd ride to work. Dropping into step with the horse we'd catch hold the hames and hotch ourselves 'UP' to sit side-saddle – with no saddle. It were a fair old hotch to land up there, but you soon got the quiff on it. It'd fall to the youngest bwoy-chap to slide down to open the gates, and the toffee-nosed carter 'ud sail through right royally, chewing his straw.

You took a pride in setting a straight furrow, often following the same line of stubble seeded with pride by the man that had trod the earth before you. You become var' close to the land and they who have toiled before when you plants your soul and plods your strength into every inch of it. A carter's reputation – and ofttimes his epitaph – be laid bare, writ in furrow and framed in 'adlands, for all the world to see, peeking over the hedgerow. And woe betide 'ee in the pub that night with they old carters if they'd spotted a dingy turnout or a skewed furrow.

We'd crane our necks likewise over the hedges of passing acres, critical, particularly of the posh estates, from our vantage seat driving the wagon to Charlbury or Woodstock.

One old carter were once 'gone right awf Blenheim 'cos the Duke of Marlborough 'adn't got 'is 'adland roight.' He must be tossin'n'turnin' in his grave at some of today's tantrum'd earth and tractor-crazy capers.

There warn't many tractors about when I started off cartering. Mr Lennox had a Titan a year or two later: a cumbersome iron-wheeled monster, viewed then as a giant 'copter in the jungle might be viewed today, wonderful useful for aiding the ground forces providing you could find an uncomplaining spot to let it down. It were a marathon task to shift it up and down the furrow; even then the ground forces, old Uncle Mont, Jolly and all had come to its aid and finish off the 'adlands. If you wanted my valuable opinion, as a fifteen-year-old carter, tractors 'ud never catch on, and the Titan were var' like to end up like that other modern marvel, the late *Titanic*.

Meanwhile us ploughed on with our Ransom or our Ball, down to earth in every sense, knowing every field, every furrow could differ from one end to the other on our big oolite soil; altering the cock according to the varying depths from the brashy banks to the rich hollows, coping with the elements, cleaning the coulters, commanding the horses, claypering our noses, boots and gaiters, until my watch said it were time for nine o'clock lunch or twelve o'clock dinner.

The nine o'clock lunch were a moveable feast, depending on which end of the furrow you'd left yer bacca; but it were politic to stick to twelve o'clock dinner for your dinner-hour, specially if the master were working with you. Twelve o'clock prompt he went home for his dinner; if you was to carry on for an extra bout he'd be back before you'd had your hour, and it'd look as if you was swinging the lead. Twelve o'clock prompt, out came the nosebags.

The youngest bwoy-chap 'ud fetch me my tucker-bag. I'd open up my tommy-cloth to find real man's grub which I yet with my real man's pocket-knife, rounded off with a drink of cold tea, and a roll of bacca for my pipe. I hadn't quite mastered a pipe when I first started cartering, but I soon got the quiff on it. Everybody smoked in they days. Over the years my pipe became my companion, a solace for long hours alone out in the fields. I 'udn't advise anybody to take it up now; smoking be a silly job, but at eighty-two I be too old to change for the better.

By the time you'd walked back and forth all day, battling with the elements, you was ready to shut off at four o'clock. They used to reckon if a chap ploughed an acre with a nine-inch-wide furrow he'd walked fourteen miles, let alone all the homping of the plough and the weight on his boots. You didn't hotch up quite so lissom on to the horse's back for the ride back to the stables. First stop – the horse-trough, to give the horses a long, long drink. How they enjoyed that end-of-work drink! They'd sink their old noses right under the water, and the level 'ud plummet like billy-o. If one had a touch of colic you'd leave the bit in his mouth so's he couldn't gollop the water so fast. Now I be carter, one of the bwoy-chaps filled the troughs. He be lucky; no more thirteen hundred 'pumps'; by now there were piped water brought overland from Spelsbury to the Fulwell farm buildings. Only to the farm buildings, not to the cottages. On the farm, animals comes first.

*Sheila Stewart,* Lifting the Latch: A Life on the Land, *1987*

As the sky darkens and the air somehow feels crisper and fresher than usual, everything becomes clearer and my ears tune in to the sound of the tiny taps of rain on the windows. Birds take shelter and the wind picks up, causing a tornado of crumpled leaves to swoop round the garden. Like the vegetable soup warming on the hob, a storm is brewing – and the first signs of it are showing.

To me, a winter storm means only one thing: the following day I have to be down at Cockerham Sands to see what treasures have been washed ashore. A full moon highlights the streams of clouds tumbling over its face. I watch them float away, knowing greater ones are yet to come, saturated with water, ready to be wrung out over the county. I cannot wait to be out on the beach uncovering the ocean's secrets.

The last time I was there I found a message in a wine bottle, the only one I've ever found. Although it was only a phone number – Polish I later discovered – written on a cigarette packet, my imagination ran wild. Who were the people or person who enjoyed this wine? Where were they going, and what were they going for? When did they throw it into the waves? Seaweed was starting to grow on the top of the bottle, which now stands on one of my shelves.

One of my favourite finds is an orange rock. It doesn't seem very special at first, but when you look closer its purpose is revealed. A ridge runs around the edge of the rock, with two dents at opposite ends. On top, contrasting with the orange appearance, is a blue, sheeny ammonite, but the fossil isn't the interesting part. The indentations were caused by a rope, so this rock is an ancient fishing weight – and that is truly fascinating.

The daily tides cause the landscape to change constantly, making each of my visits different and continually surprising. Nature can be mysterious in some ways. We only really tend to see the bigger picture, rarely noticing the smaller pixels. We mainly see nature scurrying on land or soaring high on warm thermals; we don't often get a chance to see what is below sea level. Storms give us a small yet fascinating opportunity to glimpse this un-touched, marine world. The seas become rougher. The waves to the underwater garden are like the wind to the leaves. Churned up material is left stranded among the pebbles as the seas calm and the tide retreats. It's hard to believe this quiet little part of More-cambe Bay was a place that no one would venture only a day ago. But now the landscape has cooled down, all returns to normal.

As the air chills, I warm up the soup and take it in a flask on my journey. With a bag in my hand and wellies on my feet, I slow-ly pace down the beach, searching for new discoveries. Binoculars and my camera are in my backpack and the trapped air between it and my coat keeps my back warm as I stumble across the shore. The warmth quickly escapes when I take off my bag to prepare the soup. Tightly holding the mug in my gloved hands I pause and take a slow and relieving sip, and instantly feel the temperature change. Exhaling a small cloud of mist I relax into this ever-changing environment, softening my shoulders and feeling the warmth spread through my body. I look up and see a huddle of oyster-catchers standing on a muddy rock. They've noticed I'm here. I take a step to continue my walk and as I do so they rise up, peep-ing to one another and flying out to sea towards the lighthouse.

Cascades of dunlin land on the bug-filled seaweed, eager for an easy, filling meal. There are mermaid purses littering the tide line, the egg cases of small spotted catshark and thornback rays. I scavenge a few, along with the fragile shells of sea urchins and a masked crab carapace. Some painted feathers of golden plover go into my bag, along with the broken skull of a guillemot. There's so much that has been washed up in a matter of 100 metres, and I know there has to be more along my mile-long coastal walk.

Ahead of me a large, lifeless bird lies among the seaweed. Pink-footed geese migrate to this coast in October from places like Iceland and Greenland, and it seems so sad that they fly all that way yet some, like this one, fail to make it back to their breeding ground in April. But it gives me the opportunity to look at this species in more detail. The first thing I notice are its pink feet; it really does live up to its name. Then its tough feathers. It's hard to believe that these quills and barbs enabled it to fly all those miles.

Further on I kick over a large rock and sandhoppers spring out in all directions to find a new and undisturbed resting place. They make me jump at first, but then I bend down and watch them as they hop with ease over stones many times their own size. It's like being a giant in a world I can't physically experience, but being able to watch this other dimension makes me feel I belong.

The unmistakable calls of peewits fill the air as I return to the car. In my heart I'm still full of joy even though I have to go home. The new memories created from a walk lasting a couple of hours will stay with me and I shall be reminded of them every time I look at the marine treasures lining my shelves.

*Sophie Bagshaw, 2016*

Take a winter stroll in fenland beneath the bank at Welney Wildfowl and Wetlands Trust (WWT) and you are walking in the footsteps of a giant, the patron saint of conservation. Peter Scott first came to the Fens of eastern England in the winter of 1927 from his base at nearby Trinity College, Cambridge, where he was a student. He came here to shoot wildfowl, and was immediately captivated by this vast open landscape dominated by productive agricultural land dotted with settlements on raised ground, framed by regimented drainage ditches and dykes, interspersed with small pockets of remnant primitive fenland, washes and reedbeds. It would shape one part of his destiny, one part of his geographical story. The skies are big here, very big, and never more so than on a crisp cloudless winter's day with a blue sky draped over the vista like a blanket from horizon to horizon. This is certainly wild, but it is not a wilderness.

The Fens are, in most part, wholly artificial, an industrial drained landscape, forged for centuries by human hand and imagination; founded upon layers of human endeavour battling with an element – water: to control it, channel it, harness it and remove it rapidly from the landscape. Land born from water. Yet, to be exposed to winter fenland is to feel the rawness of an east wind racing in off the North Sea, to feel an overwhelming sense of cold bleak wildness.

Scott spent much of his university spare time wildfowling on the washlands, moving to live at Borough Fen Decoy in

1932 and then buying a lighthouse in 1933 at Sutton Bridge, where the straightened River Nene rushes into The Wash. Here he started a modest personal collection of pinioned ducks and geese. Visitors now come to Welney in the winter armed with binoculars, telescopes and cameras. When Peter Scott first walked this landscape – before he tamed it, understood it and its wildlife, and came to see its grand beauty – he was armed with a shotgun.

We underestimate how powerful the hunting impulse has been in the past in stimulating conservation thinking, how powerful the voyage from guns to binoculars can be for a reflective romantic mind in tune with nature. The 'repentant butcher' has been a pivotal character in changing scientific and public attitudes, in securing environmental legislation and in founding nature protection organisations. Scott is our best exemplar; a wildfowler who went on to be the loudest conservation voice arguing for the protection of migrating ducks and geese and wet places, and who set up home at what was then named the Severn Wildfowl Trust, later the Wildfowl Trust, at Slimbridge in Gloucestershire in 1946. It took on its wider remit in 1989, recognising the enduring links between nature, people and place (habitat) by changing its name to the Wildfowl and Wetlands Trust.

In the winter of 1966–67, at a time of emerging public concern for the environment, Peter Scott returned to the Fens. This time he had a very different vision of place: first to survey the winter wildfowl and waders feeding and roosting on the washes around Welney, and then to set up a refuge to offer them protection both from disturbance and shooting. He wisely turned to Josh Scott, a local fenman steeped in the tradition of both harvesting and manipulating this wet world for human gain. He asked him to set aside killing, to forever beach his punt-gun and to use his innate connection to the Hundred Foot Washes complex to become its protector: in 1968 the washes had their first warden. The Welney Wetland Centre opened to the public in the winter of 1970, reflecting Peter Scott's central desire for his organisation to encourage close contact between people and nature. Over 46,000 visitors now come here annually, the majority between November and March, for (unlike most British wildlife attractions) Welney is far busier with people in the winter months than in the summer.

They come to see a real swan lake, a kaleidoscope of birds in front of a heated swan observatory complete with comfy sofas: winter ecotourism deluxe. Migrant whooper swans from Iceland mingle with shyer Bewick's swans in from Siberia, and cranky resident mute swans from just down the road that seem to resent the invasion by their yellow-billed cousins from the north. Vast flocks of male pochard from Eastern Europe (the clever females have gone to Spain for the winter) jostle for position with other colourful duck visitors from colder climes: wigeon, tufted duck, mallard, teal and pintail. The main lagoon hosts staged wild swan feeds with commentary three times a day; one is hauntingly ethereal under floodlights in the evenings. It's a win-win situation. The tourists are kept warm and engagingly close to the birds and the swans get a supplementary feed to the wild food they find out on neighbouring farm fields, which makes them fitter and stronger. In the harshest winters, these feeds are life-saving. WWT gets valuable publicity, promotion of its work and endless membership recruitment opportunities. Back in the winter of 1964, WWT scientists at Slimbridge pioneered the study of individual Bewick's swan bill patterns to identify (and christen) returning birds. Naming nature like this allows generational stories of swan romance, intrigue, scandal and triumph to enliven our winter doldrums. We all love a good sexy soap opera.

I met Sir Peter Scott (he had been knighted in 1973, the first ever for 'services to conservation') just once, as a pimply over-excited teenage naturalist in the summer of 1985 at Martin Mere WWT in Lancashire, my county of fledgling nature exploration. He signed a book for me. I treasure it. Whenever I walk along the banks around Welney, overlooking the Ouse Washes, that remarkable linear framed landscape of water and sky, watching wild swans fly into and out of the safety of the observatory's main lagoon, like waves of scheduled aircraft arriving and departing a busy airport, I call to mind the enormous debt of gratitude that we modern wildlife enthusiasts, who cherish nature and wild places in our crowded islands, owe the founding visionaries of this now mass conservation movement. Peter Scott lives on in the winter wonderland that is Welney.

*Dr Rob Lambert, 2016*

## The House Beautiful

A naked house, a naked moor,
A shivering pool before the door,
A garden bare of flowers and fruit
And poplars at the garden foot:
Such is the place that I live in,
Bleak without and bare within.

Yet shall your ragged moor receive
The incomparable pomp of eve,
And the cold glories of dawn
Behind your shivering trees be drawn;
And when the wind from place to place
Doth the unmoored cloud-galleons chase,
Your garden gloom and gleam again,
With leaping sun, with glancing rain.
Here shall the wizard moon ascend
The heavens, in the crimson end
Of day's declining splendour; here
The army of the stars appear.

The neighbour hollows dry or wet,
Spring shall with tender flowers beset;
And oft the morning muser see
Larks rising from the broomy lea,

*And every fairy wheel and thread*
*Of cobweb dew-bediamonded.*
*When daisies go, shall winter time*
*Silver the simple grass with rime;*
*Autumnal frosts enchant the pool*
*And make the cart-ruts beautiful;*
*And when snow-bright the moor expands,*
*How shall your children clap their hands!*
*To make this earth our hermitage,*
*A cheerful and a changeful page,*
*God's bright and intricate device*
*Of days and seasons doth suffice.*

*Robert Louis Stevenson, 1887*

*The* lights go out.

You think you know where Shetland is, but do you really? We're the afterthought on the TV weather map, we're Fair Isle on the shipping forecast, we're part of the UK but they say our nearest railway station is in Norway. We're as far north as Anchorage and St Petersburg. In summer, we enjoy almost twenty-one hours of daylight. And in winter . . . the lights go out. Daylight drains from the sky, clouds stream in from the Atlantic, and the grass becomes dull and brown. The islands brace themselves to weather what's coming.

The mountain hares in the depths of the hills are suddenly shockingly white against the russet heather. Wildfowl from far away pitch down on the lochs, great northern divers lurk half-submerged in shallow bays, and eiders congregate in tight, seething flocks in tidal voes. White-winged glaucous and Iceland gulls appear in Lerwick, the islands' small capital, patrolling the waterfront for scraps of fish from Scottish trawlers in for shelter and a night in a bright, warm pub for the crew. Grey seals hang in the dark water beside the rust-streaked hulls, reflections of the waterfront dancing in their wide black eyes.

*The lights go out.*

It's late January and bitterly cold. The streetlights abruptly extinguish, and a ripple of anticipation passes through the crowds lining the roads in the centre of Lerwick. A heartbeat later and a maroon hisses high overhead to explode with deafening violence above us. The old stone houses on the brow of the hill glow briefly blood-red as flares are lit at their feet – and then they are golden, lit brightly by a thousand flaming torches held overhead by the guizers of Up Helly Aa.

This is our fire festival, our nod to our Scandinavian fore-bears. This is the bearded, chain-mailed, axe-wielding, defiant fuck-you to winter's endless darkness. This is a Viking roar into the night. The raven banner flies all over town, blood-red and black, snapping in the icy, keening wind.

'We axe for what we want.'

The play on words is knowing – the guizer jarl, his thick beard heavily streaked with salty grey, leads the procession of men through the town. Each carries a flaming brand overhead, following their leader and the wooden longboat built specially for this moment. They have waited a year since they last con-signed a longboat to a vortex of flames; the jarl himself has waited a lifetime for this day.

The longboat comes to a halt. Surrounded by a wheeling kaleidoscope of torches the jarl stands proudly in the boat. 'Three cheers for Up Helly Aa!' The answering roar from a thousand guizers at his feet echoes off the houses around us. His winged helmet is backlit by dancing fire, flames playing on the engraved blade of the axe he holds proudly overhead. This is his moment.

He rejoins his men and the flaming torches begin to fly. They come slowly at first, and then faster and faster, thrown from all sides into the bowels of the longboat. The carved dragon's head at the prow rises from a maelstrom of fire. You can feel the heat on your face. Suddenly the Shetland night isn't so cold after all.

*The lights go out.*

The longboat burns out quickly, leaving just a pool of glowing embers to mark its passing. The jarl and the guizers have all gone now, away to spend the night drinking and dancing with the townsfolk in a party that will last to dawn, pause for a cooked breakfast and then return to the pubs for another night.

Away from town the stars are achingly bright overhead. The moon is just a sliver in the sky, and to the north the aurora borealis appears: a dull glow on the very horizon at first, but then flaring into smoky bluish-green towers and streaks that cover half the dome of stars above us. The sky pulsates overhead – it is as if we can see the heartbeat of the universe itself. The Vikings were said to have believed these shimmering lights were the reflections off the armour and shields of the Valkyries, the female warriors who welcomed the fallen into Valhalla. The Shetland descendants of those Vikings simply call them the *mirrie dancers* – a gentler name for a more peaceful time.

With such visible, electric drama it feels as if there should be some sound, some fizzing or static hiss to match the lights ... but there is nothing, just the constant sea mouthing at the shore in the distance. The stars and the aurora cast enough light for us to make our way without a torch, and we walk quietly beneath the drama in the heavens above, our breath spooling behind us in phosphorescent puffs.

We reach a small loch beside the narrow road that leads to our house. An opaque sheet of milky ice sheathes it, and somewhere out there whooper swans bugle nervously at the sound of our approach. Their hearing is far better than our sight – they know we're coming before we can make out their dim forms. There are two gleaming white adults and two, maybe three greyer forms in the gloom – a family party freshly arrived from

Iceland. The ice creaks and groans beneath them as they walk unhurriedly away from us towards the far shore.

The smell of peat smoke is sweet in the air as we climb the track to our whitewashed crofthouse. We left the fire burning while we were watching the Up Helly Aa procession and the house will be warm for our return. A guttering candle on the kitchen windowsill welcomes us home. The aurora has peaked with shifting blossoms of light overhead fading into the north as quickly as they came. The Valkyries have swept back to their distant halls, and the stars have the sky to themselves once more. We step inside to drink hot, sweet tea and rub life back into deadened hands. I snuff the candle's flame between nerveless thumb and forefinger as I prepare for what's left of another long Shetland winter night.

*The lights go out.*

*Jon Dunn, 2016*

## February–March

**Feb. 6.**    Ravens carry over materials & seem to be building. *Footnote.* Foxes begin now to be very rank, & to smell so high, that as one rides along of a morning it is easy to distinguish where they have been the night before. At this season the intercourse between the sexes commences; & the females intimate their wants to the males by three or four little sharp yelpings or barkings frequently repeated. This anecdote I learned by living formerly by an house opposite to a neighbour that kept a tame bitch fox, which every spring about candlemas began her amorous serenade as soon as it grew dark, & continued it nightly thro' y$^e$ months of Feb. & March. The wheat this year looks very weak & poor; last winter it was proud and gay; & yet after a cold wet summer the crop was very indifferent. Farmer Lassam feeds his early lambs, & their ewes with oats & bran: the lambs are large & fat.

**Feb. 15.**    The sun at setting shines into the E. corner of my great parlor.

**Feb. 19.**    The dry air crisps my plaster in the new parlor.

**Mar. 2.**    [Farnham] Snow in the night, sun, & mild.

**Mar. 3–12.** [South Lambeth] Turkey-cock struts & gobbles.

**Mar. 7.**    Rain, harsh & dark, much London smoke.

*Reverend Gilbert White, The Naturalist's Journal, 1778*

## The Darkling Thrush

I leant upon a coppice gate
    When Frost was spectre-grey,
And Winter's dregs made desolate
    The weakening eye of day.
The tangled bine-stems scored the sky
    Like strings of broken lyres,
And all mankind that haunted nigh
    Had sought their household fires.

The land's sharp features seemed to be
    The Century's corpse outleant,
His crypt the cloudy canopy,
    The wind his death-lament.
The ancient pulse of germ and birth
    Was shrunken hard and dry,
And every spirit upon earth
    Seemed fervourless as I.

At once a voice arose among
    The bleak twigs overhead
In a full-hearted evensong
    Of joy illimited;
An aged thrush, frail, gaunt, and small,
    In blast-beruffled plume,

*Had chosen thus to fling his soul*
*Upon the growing gloom.*

*So little cause for carolings*
*Of such ecstatic sound*
*Was written on terrestrial things*
*Afar or nigh around,*
*That I could think there trembled through*
*His happy good-night air*
*Some blessed Hope, whereof he knew*
*And I was unaware.*

*Thomas Hardy, 1900*

S altmarshes in winter are lifeless places – grey-brown, forbidding, bleak. A handful of little egrets stand like sentinels here and there; a short-eared owl flaps lazily past. In summer this place would be bursting with song and life and colour: now all is still and hushed. The horizon blurs as the pale sky relinquishes what little colour it has gleaned from today's weak, watery sun. You're waiting for a ghost to appear.

Ten minutes to four. Perfect.

Up on the banking you're exposed. Winter is about endurance and that's all you can do. Endure. Fingers numbed from the frostbitten breeze, cheeks red and raw and burning from the cold; you blink to stop your eyes from watering.

Then, without pomp or fanfare, the spectre appears unannounced, materialising from the marsh. Gliding on shallow v-shaped wings, the hen harrier moves with the muscular elegance of a male ballet dancer; strong, purposeful and full of grace.

You are unseen or disregarded; your presence on the bank is irrelevant. The grey body is hard to clearly define in the gloaming, but the flight is unmistakable. The ashy head scans left to right, patrolling its domain; you can't see the piercing yellow eyes, but they're alert and watchful. From above, the rump glows, a patch of pure white snow and the splayed wing tips – five fingers pointing skyward – look as if they've been dipped in ink.

The silver apparition haunts the saltmarsh, subtle, silent yet omnipotent. Suddenly it banks sharply around, hovers for a moment and then drops, melting into the fading landscape. It doesn't reappear. A few minutes pass but the phantom has departed to another world, leaving nothing more than an impression, a memory. Pack up and leave: the ghost has gone.

*Lucy McRobert, 2016*

The Primaveral Season begins about Candlemas. The increasing day is now sensibly longer, and the lighter evenings begin to be remarked by the absence of candles till near six o'clock. The weather is generally milder, and the exception to this rule, or a frosty Candlemas day, is found so generally to be indicative of a cold Primaveral Period, that it has given rise to several proverbs related in the subsequent part of this work. We have all heard from our infancy the adage,

> *'If Candlemas day be fair and bright,*
> *Winter will have another flight;'*

and I find by examining journals that this is generally correct. About this time the first signs of the early spring appear in the flowering of the Snowdrops; they rise above ground, and generally begin to flower by Candlemas eve, being recorded, during the old style, in numbers about the feast of the Purification of the Virgin Mary.

*Thomas Furly Forster,* The Pocket Encyclopaedia of Natural Phenomena, *published 1827*

'As the days lengthen the cold strengthens,' is an old country saying. February brings the severe frosts and the snow. Ponds are frozen over and the village children make slides down the lanes on their way to school. The blacksmith finds that people pause and enter his smithy for a gossip, that they may thaw themselves near his fire; and there is something particularly welcome about the warm smell of new bread from the bakehouse.

Old Mrs Quex has three oil stoves alight in the village shop, but still her fingers let the knife slip as she cuts the cheese or the bacon. When the bellringers gather together for practice in the church in the evenings, there is a loud beating of arms and hands to bring blood back into finger tips.

But while the sun glows low and red above the frozen fields there is shelter and comparative warmth in the coppice. Here men are busy felling the undergrowth. Black they look against the thin covering of shining snow on the ground, all varieties of colour lost in their contrasting depth of tone. There is a pathetic lack of privacy about this white blanket laid over the earth. The clearings may be silent of rabbits during the daytime, but the patterning of the smooth surface of the snow by small pad marks, three to each rabbit, tells of animation in the crisp frosty moonlight. Since the last snow-fall in the late afternoon, there are tell-tale prints down the lane to the wood, where John has walked out with Jenny, and what the winter twilight kindly hid has been shown to the gossiping village in a trail of clustered footmarks, two big, two small. Birds forget their timidity under the urge of hunger, and hop and flutter among the feet of the woodmen. The snow is imprinted with lacy designs where they have hopped, deeper and bigger for blackbird and thrush, intermingled with the delicate signatures of chaffinch and tit.

Hedging and ditching, lopping and clearing; these are February's work, for they can be done in frost and cold, when the blade of the plough would fail to turn the hard, resisting earth, and the litter lies frozen to the farmyard, so that it cannot be carted into the fields.

The hazel undergrowth is thinned and stacked into faggots and bavins and left to 'dry out' in the coppice. Through the woods comes the sharp snapping sound of the chopping of small branches, broken occasionally by the distant boom of a falling tree. There is no quietness in the thickets just now for the little things of the earth, the rabbits and foxes and hares.

In the middle of the field down by the water mill stands a lonely scarecrow. Prominent and dark against the white of the snow-covered land, it looks a cold, pathetic object, less protection against the ravages of the birds than the snow itself which covers the lately sown grain. A missel thrush ironically sits on the 'mawkin's' weather-worn bowler hat, singing out across the still fields. The snow lodges in the straw stuffing which has broken through holes in the tattered old coat. The birds watch the field, and at the first sign of thaw they will descend upon it in a dusky cloud to pierce through the softened, melting snow and find the seed grain. Against their hunger the scarecrow stands impotent.

Gaunt willows border the mill stream. The piles of willow hurdles for the sheepfolds are wearing low. So the farmer lops.

The grim, individual shapes of the willow trees lean in a row over the black unfrozen waters of the running stream, seared and wrinkled, like a family of mourners. One by one the upspringing branches within reach from the ladder are slashed off. The lopper next stands on the platform of the tree-top, like an elongation of the dark tree itself, and chops at the few remaining branches until the last one towers alone and grotesque, like the single tooth in an old man's sunken mouth. This collapses, too, and the tree stands compact.

In the rickyard the root-hale, covered with earth and straw, is opened, and out of it tumble gleaming balls of purple and orange, their colour enriched by contrast with the dirty snow of the trodden ground. These are carted to the Big Barn and again tumbled out upon the dusty floor. Here in this shelter the men cut and slice the roots for the cattle, thankful to be away from the piercing wind on the fields. For there is no love of outdoor work just now. Eagerly the men search for those jobs that will keep them in shelter; the cow-sheds are white-washed, harness is mended and polished, traps and carts and waggons need repairing.

The days end early, and after feeding the animals in the stalls, the men go home down the lane, tripped up by the frozen ridges of the cart ruts, rosy in the setting sun. Hot meat teas await them, and long evenings of drawn curtains and pipes and dozing.

In the lofty elms of the vicarage garden the rooks, too, go home to rest, croaking loudly and solemnly as they settle into their bulgy nests in the tree-tops.

But the farmer sits throughout the long evenings in the farm kitchen, slowly and with many falterings, making out his plans for the year. There is no beginning and no end to this year of his, but the hard weather brings a pause. The oil lamp swings from the ceiling, casting giant shadows into the corners of the room. It throws a circle of light upon him and his note-book and stump of pencil that are to determine by a few scribbles on paper the face of the land through the year. By this stump of pencil is decided the fate of this calf and that sow, the rams over the hill, the bull in the barton. These badly-shaped grey letters will turn one field to grass and another to swedes, mate the grey mare, and fling the perfume of a beanfield across the land. They will form a nesting place for larks, and plough the field mouse from her home. The destiny of myriads of unhatched insects waits on the twist that red horny hand gives to his pencil. So is the pattern of the year designed out of the farmer's brain.

For days on end the steel grip of the frost holds the land. The plough lies half covered with snow; the robin hops in at the farm kitchen window. And all the time, under the coverlet of snow, the vivid green wheat grows in the fields. Soon the thaw will come, and as the dark earth is visible again in the farmhouse garden, it shall be spotted with snowdrops and the pale gold of frilled aconites.

*Clare Leighton*, The Farmer's Year:
A Calendar of English Husbandry, *1933*

The mulberry tree now stands alone in a clearing, swathed in frost, a small shrub that was once the heart of a blossoming garden, carved and cultivated by starched gardeners a hundred years before. Uprooted from Asia, it was transported by sea to bring shade to luncheons on the lawn, where guests smoked bronze tobacco with their tea and cakes and ices.

In 1854 the wood in which the mulberry stands was bisected by a railway, designed to carry passengers to that vast feat of imperial strength, the Crystal Palace. London hoarded treasures from across the globe and housed them in a glass castle: ivory, porcelain, baroque tapestries and lost elephants filled the halls; the Koh-i-Noor diamond was displayed before the gaze of the rich. Every day crowds swarmed the palace and stared at the world in cabinets, and with warmer weather, queues lengthened. A committee soon decided that an ancient woodland in Sydenham would provide a useful rail path for special excursion trains. They cut lines in the soil and filled it with tracks, ensuring no old trees would stand in the way of progress.

Soon this woodland was declared fashionable; mansions were erected between beech and birch, and people littered their gardens with rockeries and sundials of cast iron. In one, a folly was built to simulate the ruins of a monastery, and a pleasure pool was carved into the earth. Rhododendrons filled the borders of flawless lawns, a Chilean monkey puzzle was brought and a cedar of Lebanon rose alone above the canopy. The wood became a hive of gossip and merriment. Acquaintances would gather at The Hoo and homes beyond, sipping tea in the balmy afternoons of the fin de siècle. Through statuette clusters hidden in foliage, news would reach them of assassinations, colonial changes and civil conflicts; they continued to sip tea. The world war passed. The Empire was diffusing like ripples at sea.

In the year of the death of King George V, the Crystal Palace was struck by a catastrophe from which it never recovered. A fire broke out, and high winds fanned flames over the walls of the palace and through parched timber frames. Dusty artefacts from ancient civilisations vanished in minutes, and by dawn the glass house had been consumed by fire. Winston Churchill called it the end of an age; and it was the end of high society in the Great North Wood. With nobody to carry, the railway soon closed and the tunnel was shut. The seven mansions of Sydenham were neglected, and by 1980 had been demolished.

Seasons changed; silence crept over the woodland. Old tracks embedded in the earth rusted through, tangerine metal fusing with soil. The folly started to crumble and the rhododendrons grew wild among the trees. Without footsteps and fanfare, the wild wood began to reveal itself.

It is winter now. Beneath the trees city workers walk their dogs and check the news on smartphones, stopping here and there to read signboards about the wild creatures that live in the wood around them. Along the track where engines used to run, the ground lies undisturbed and carpeted with fungi: candle-snuff, oysterling, birch polypore, coral spot and clouded funnel. As the light fades, night-time creatures emerge: woodpeckers and bats flit between branches, the last nuthatch seeks a bed, a fox leaves her den and wood mice search for tender roots in the fallen leaves.

The woodland continues to thrive in the winter, yet the mulberry, once a specimen of exotic allure, stands limp in the clearing, its branches home to a hundred woodlice. The night is quiet as birds and mammals sleep; an old tawny owl shuffles on top of a silver birch tree, and one black eye peers out across the forest. The treetops lie before him like a lagoon. The eye closes; his soft plumes rustle in the breeze, warming his mortal heart against the cold.

*Tiffany Francis, 2016*

## Muckraker

In February the water-troughs grew
thick grey rinds, ice that looked like frozen
foam you could break with a blow from the haft
of a mucking-out shovel. The milk-cows,
Guernseys and Jerseys, drank, swirling pale spit
with brown rust-water. Their muzzles trailed strands
of thick, pearly white that looked beautiful
if you could divorce them from their context.
Divorced from the context of the orphanage,
this farm was as beautiful as the cows
who pressed their huge flanks against my body,
forgetting (or unaware) that I was
small and very human. They had the eyes
of post-coital women; wide and so black
you could see your secret thoughts rising up
through those pools. You could scry your own future.
Standing there, hungry, stroking their coarse flanks,
my jaw swollen, fractured beneath livid
skin, I thought that all I saw was just one
more fantasy: a warm bed, piles of books,
a naked, broad-shouldered man I wasn't
afraid of. A man who'd never worked on
a farm, or stuck his thing where it wasn't
wanted. I drew back, sharp, when a young milker

*leaned forward to nuzzle me. At this point*
*tenderness could only bring forth pain. I*
*slipped in three inches of part-frozen shit.*
*The sharp scent rose when I fractured the crust.*
*I braced myself with the blade of the scoop.*
*After a while, I went back to shovelling.*

*Bethany Pope, 2016*

After a week of wet, blustery weather, most of which we've spent huddling by the fire in our draughty old house, it's a joy to get outside, despite the cold.

St Catherine's Hill rises steeply above the River Itchen on the outskirts of Winchester. Owned by Winchester College, and managed by the Hampshire & Isle of Wight Wildlife Trust, this place intrigues me. It hugs the city on one side, and is hemmed in by the noisy M3 on another, yet as we climb the muddy path from the car park it quickly feels as if we're leaving civilisation behind. For some, the thrum of traffic is an intrusion, something against which protesters battled before the motorway was built in the 1990s. But for me, as we ascend, the sound rolls like waves on a beach, soothing rather than distracting, harmonising with the hum of the wind as we get higher.

Slipping on last year's leaves, we follow a narrow track which curls towards the summit of the hill until our way is blocked by a trio of small creamy cows, their breath steaming in the cold air. They look bigger, close up. One turns to look at us over her shoulder, soft liquid eyes unconcerned by our presence. She obligingly side-steps a metre or so, flicking her tail playfully as I squeeze past. My scarf whips in the wind and snags on the ragged hawthorn hedge, leaving a strand of pink wool to decorate its bare branches. The cow resumes her meal with her companions, tugging at a tussock of tufty grass, and we continue on our way.

At the top, I'm surprised when we emerge on to a broad expanse of well-cropped turf. Cattle and ponies are put out to graze here to control the scrub which would otherwise rapidly reclaim the chalky downland. In a few months, a carpet of herbs and wildflowers will burst from the thin soil, attracting thousands of butterflies including chalkhill blues and marbled whites, but for now there is little colour in the winter landscape. Everything seems washed out, grey-brown like a sepia photograph.

The grassy plateau is dotted with rabbit droppings and a spaniel runs in delirious circles in the endless space, delighted to be released from the tight confines of the hedgerow-lined path. We see neither cows nor ponies up here, and once the dog has led its owners away we are alone on the windswept hilltop. Below us, the Itchen Navigation looks strangely out of place – a stretch of water domesticated into a ruler-straight canal, while the untamed river meanders alongside. The chalk stream of the Itchen, and the water meadows which line its banks, offer homes to otters and kingfishers, crayfish and water-rail, all surviving on the fringe of this ancient city. The wildlife has had plenty of time to adapt to humans. The Romans founded Winchester, naming it Belgarum, and King Alfred the Great, whose statue stands guard outside the Guildhall, made it the Saxon capital. It is an appealing and historic city, but the best view is up here on 'St Cath's'.

The only trees on the hill are a coppice of beeches, which huddle at the highest point, 97 metres above sea level. Somewhere in this silent wood, where the wind hushes, lie the buried ruins of St Catherine's chapel. Built in Norman times, nothing of it remains above ground, its stones carried off long ago; but perhaps the quiet spirits of the nuns remain.

Far older, yet more visible, are signs of Iron Age habitation. This exposed hill offered the perfect site for a fort, with steep ridges which were easy to defend and views for miles across the Hampshire countryside. Ramparts and ditches were dug into the contours of the hill, changing the outline of the landscape for ever. Only a determined and resourceful invader could attack this place unseen. It was these early settlers who cleared the trees for livestock, and centuries-old paths criss-cross the slopes where sheep were driven to market. This wasn't just a fort, it was a gathering place, perhaps for religious reasons, perhaps merely social, but thousands of people have climbed this hill before us. If I believed in ghosts, I might hear their voices in the wind. And what of the Roman legionnaires who camped here, or Cromwell's militia in the Civil War? All have left their mark.

It's too cold to stand daydreaming for long, although the dark clouds which had blown in from the coast have given way to feathery white ones against a fragile blue sky. We follow a path downhill, making our way towards the river and the town. Plague pits lie hidden in this valley, a grim reminder of the multitudes who died in Winchester in the 1660s and were carted here to be buried in mass graves. I shiver, despite the emerging sunshine. The Itchen looks blue now, the sky reflected in its shallow waters, and the flint walls of St Cross Hospital and its Almshouse of Noble Poverty, the oldest charitable institution in England, rise on the opposite bank. Oddly, there is a wooden stairway down the southern slope. One hundred steps lead steeply down towards the water meadows, ending abruptly, so that I must leap from the last step as if jumping from a moving escalator.

'I'm winning!' a voice behind me shouts.

Three teenage girls, all in skinny jeans and multi-coloured trainers, barrel past us, shrieking and giggling as they slide down the grassy bank. They race to hug the trunk of a stunted, storm-battered tree, faces flushed and glowing. Their windswept energy is infectious. Risking the disapproval of ghostly nuns, I abandon middle-aged dignity, and run, grinning, to the bottom of the hill.

*Claire Thurlow, 2016*

How long the winter has been in going! Winters are always long; but some of them seem to us much longer than they ought to be, owing to a lengthy spell of north-east winds filling the sky with dark, heavy cloud, when we are longing to see the swaying tassels of the hazel, the golden stars of lesser celandine and the haloes of the leafless coltsfoot; to hear the welcome call of cuckoo and the rippling song of nightingale.

To town-folk the winter always appears much longer than it does to dwellers in the country; these, being on the spot, can take a fair ramble during the eight or nine hours of daylight, making up for the scarcity of flowers and insects by watching for those birds that are with us only during the winter. There are, also, the shrews and mice in the hedge-bottom, and their hunters the stoat and weasel, to take note of; as well as glimpses of squirrels and the occasional bat that has woke up for a brief flight. There are almost endless treasures to be found in the pond, as soon as the thick ice has melted and made them easy to see and reach; and there are some things, such as many of the mosses, that can be found in full beauty during the cooler, moister months only.

*Edward Step,* Nature Rambles: An Introduction to Country-lore, *1930*

There's a sudden movement off to my left. A pale shape, only just visible. I slowly turn my head, but instead of the expected grazing sheep I see a mountain hare, his white winter coat standing out against the brown mountain grasses. A twitch of his black-tipped ears and he turns to run off to the higher and wilder moorland. This, just a few hundred metres from the Woodhead road, one of the busiest Pennine passes.

The Longdendale Valley lies in the borderland between Derbyshire and Yorkshire, its series of Victorian reservoirs providing water to the people of Tameside and Greater Manchester. Winter rains pour down from the Pennines towards the River Etherow and keep the reservoirs at respectable levels. The Pennine Way crosses the valley from Bleaklow to the Black Hill, a relief perhaps to those who find the boggy moors a heavy start on their first day out from Edale. Many underestimate the tough conditions of Pennine walking and focus their attention solely on putting one foot in front of the other until they get the day over. Not many take the time to observe the creatures who make the high moors their home. It only needs a few steps off the path on Kinder to reach the places where the hares run, or where they lie in their shallow forms to rest.

I've lived in the Longdendale Valley for nearly twenty years now. The Peak District begins a couple of fields behind my house so that an evening stroll takes me from the village into the National Park. Within minutes I leave the concerns of daily life behind and enter the natural world, listening to the lapwings and curlews or watching a shrew scurrying across my path into the undergrowth, safe from the eye of a hunting tawny owl. Often in the dusk I see a brown hare startling out of the meadow and racing across the fields to find safer ground.

From my kitchen window I see the mound of Peak Naze and watch the changing seasons reflected in its colours; the lush greens of early spring growth or the smattering of light winter snow on the tops in January. Sometimes the hillside glows golden in the sunset or disappears altogether into the morning mists of autumn. The hill is named for its shape as it forms a narrow protrusion at the end of Bleaklow, nosing towards Glossop. From the top there are wonderful open landscapes on three sides and gently rolling moors heading up to Bleaklow on the other. There is a rocky outcrop to sit and enjoy the views. Someone has scrawled 'Be Free' across the stones and this is truly a place to find freedom. Walking up here in all weathers and from all directions I've become familiar with the call of skylarks rising from the grass and the curlews' burbling cry. This is grouse country and there are many of them here, their ungainly flight and jarring call marking their presence when disturbed.

This landscape has been strongly shaped by human activities. There are numerous disused quarries, the stone from which built the nearby houses and mills in the heyday of the industrial revolution. My own small village was home to four mills at one time, although it now seems impossible that little Padfield Brook could have ever run fast enough to power them all. Following around the ridge from Peak Naze you eventually come across a large area of abandoned quarry faces and ruined buildings. The walls provide welcome shelter from the bitter winds that blow across the hills in the winter and I've been happy to settle my back against them while I pause for a rest and a bite to eat. I've often seen signs of hares here and imagine a night camped nearby would give ample opportunities to watch them. Hares tend to be solitary creatures and I'm accustomed to seeing them one at a time, usually as they run away from me across the moors; but one wintry afternoon I disturbed a group of hares in the middle of these empty ruins and mounds of half-cut stones. Brown hares, I think, although at a distance I can find them hard to distinguish from their mountain cousins. The common hares are a little larger, their black-tipped ears slightly longer and a mountain hare's tail remains white all year round, but brief sightings don't always provide clear views of these identifying features. However, once the daylight length shifts sufficiently towards wintertime, the mountain hares change into their snowy white winter coat and become completely unmistakeable.

One February morning, I saw from my kitchen window that Peak Naze was covered in a deep layer of fresh snow. Clear blue skies tempted me away from the comfort of my cottage and suitably bundled in my winter clothing I headed for the hills. I had no clear path in mind other than to enjoy the day, my footsteps clearly visible behind me and a smooth spread of snow in front. When the choice came between continuing ahead to join the Pennine Way or turning right to the old quarries, I paused to look back and admire the view. Turning around, I noticed the distinctive tracks of a hare in the snow to my left and thought I'd follow them across the moors. Over a stile and dropping into a deep drift, I was envious of the hare's ability to run over the top of the snow. I know this terrain and was well aware of the dips and mounds normally obscured by heather and now even more so by a foot and more of snow. I stumbled along following the tracks, wishing I'd bothered to get the gaiters out of my pack as packed snow rapidly filled my boots and worked its way under my waterproof trousers.

Near here are buildings used by scientists who manage areas of this moorland to assess its ability to recover from industrial pollution. The hare had been here before me, and as I struggled to get up from yet another fall into the snow, I became aware of him sitting quietly watching me; his coat the colour of snow, his black-tipped ears and dark eyes following my movements. Had I not been following his tracks I would probably have missed him, his colouring the perfect disguise for the day. It is ironic perhaps that the snowy conditions that hide him most effectively are also those that betray his passing. The next flurry would hide his tracks and start to fill the bigger marks of my unsteady feet. I headed back down to the valley, leaving my mountain hare to his wintry home.

*Ann MacCarthy, 2016*

It was about the beginning of the spring 1757 when I arrived in England, and I was near twelve years of age at that time. I was very much struck with the buildings and the pavement of the streets in Falmouth; and, indeed, any object I saw filled me with new surprise. One morning, when I got upon deck, I saw it covered all over with the snow that fell over-night: as I had never seen any thing of the kind before, I thought it was salt; so I immediately ran down to the mate, and desired him, as well as I could, to come and see how somebody in the night had thrown salt all over the deck. He, knowing what it was, desired me to bring some of it down to him: accordingly I took up a handful of it, which I found very cold indeed; and when I brought it to him he desired me to taste it. I did so, and I was surprised beyond measure. I then asked him what it was; he told me it was snow: but I could not in any wise understand him. He asked me if we had no such thing in my country? and I told him, No. I then asked him the use of it, and who made it; he told me a great man in the heavens, called God: but here again I was to all intents and purposes at a loss to understand him; and the more so, when a little after I saw the air filled with it, in a heavy shower, which fell down on the same day.

*Olaudah Equiano,* The Interesting Narrative
of the Life of Olaudah Equiano, *1789*

*Fret:*
1. *to feel or express worry, annoyance, discontent*
2. *to make a way by gnawing, corrosion, wearing away, etc.*
3. *to move in agitation or commotion, as water*
4. *a fog or mist*

February. Walled in cold. We wonder at the sky, an ash-grey ceiling of clouds – low and lowering. I had suffered a period of lethargy and distress, manifesting in what felt like a flutter of dancing moth-breaths in the chest. I needed to feel the roll of the land, to exercise, to *exorcise*. I had been speaking to my sister, now resident in the States – a mile closer to the sun, in Colorado. She'd spoken of the things she missed: the long bronze twilights and the steady blaze of autumn, the procession of lime trees along the back road, an ever-present thick-kneed colonnade joining versions of self to self. But most of all? Most of all, now she was bleached in the thin dry mountain air, she missed the simple fact of invisible water: that close-cloak of moist air we never see, but which we carry on us like a second skin, unnoticed until it's gone.

Water-divining dreams came. We awoke the next day to find the world had shrunk: a wall of mist, a fistful of houses, the road choked at its gizzard; the huge oak, our boundary tree, whose crown was usually one of our vaulting points to heaven, was headless, stunted, smothered with a scurf of off-white linen. Dirty drifts of hanging moisture moved in slow processions across rooftops. The sky was falling. A day for hiding, not walking. Which, anyway, might just be the same thing. I decided to head out.

The drive to Old Winchester Hill was gloomy: studying minute shifts in cloud-hue, frowning at the blue-bleak horizon, watching for rain. I'd encased myself in an outer shell of waterproof clothing, and even sitting still I was creating my own rubberised, rustling symphony. This was absurd, but already set in motion. I'd apparently been sleepwalking the preceding night, looking through the curtains, setting things in order, my mind churning. Now we were here, and the landscape was nothing but a rumour.

Standing due south of the old fort at Winchester Hill, squinting into the hanging air, it's improbably quiet. A while ago I stood here, swaying gently towards the falling away of the land, the loamy country impossibly variegated and plural, tumbling over itself to the limits of vision. Today, I see less than 50 yards. Mist has reduced the hills to another room – a vast room hung with clammy drapes, drapes that consume light and deaden sound. Out in the open and moving, the land opens up a bit. There are new ways of seeing through the veils, new sonic possibilities: a nuthatch throws its pulsing liquid missiles; a green woodpecker laughs into the void. Close up, everything is pin-sharp: primroses clustered around a fence post; a rain-blackened stand of ancient hollow-stemmed umbellifers; clotted, contorted beech trunks, carrying tiny runnels of collected moisture.

Butser Hill is the highest point of the South Downs, and I am in clouds. Wreathed in humid folds. I consider, as I walk, that I'm a cloud-gatherer, expelling and absorbing the fret as I move; an alveolus for moisture exchange. Beneath me the ground is slick and broken, a gradually unfolding puzzle of mud and exposed flint and chalk. Sickly flowering gorse reefs loom and fade, crouched and arthritic like abandoned trench defences. In the further reaches of the acoustic shadows, I hear the A3. It should be a toxic roar, but it feels half-fictional, its harsh sibilance reduced to a bristle-tongued whisper. It limns the visible world, pulls at the feet. I know I have to cross so I start to descend, following the eastward curve of a widening greenway.

I ford the A3, and beyond, on the beech-clad scarp of the Queen Elizabeth Country Park, the mist starts to lift. With it, I notice a soft de-cloaking and, despite the gradient of the hanger, with the opening up, with the redrawing of the land, my breath eases. I crash through massive piles of beech leaves and feel the canopy above coming alive. I stop, and notice, ten metres away, a wood pigeon quite still beside the path. I crouch and watch the steady pulse of its breathing. It doesn't appear in distress and as I inch closer I think I could gather it up, but instead I simply sit and conspire, breathing again, breathing again, breathing again.

*Matt Poacher, 2016*

## *Sonnet XLVIII*

*Like as the thrush in winter, when the skies*
*Are drear and dark and all the woods are bare,*
*Sings undismayed, till from his melodies*
*Odours of spring float through the frozen air; –*
*So in my heart, when sorrow's icy breath*
*Is bleak and bitter and its frost is strong,*
*Leaps up, defiant of despair and death,*
*A sunlit fountain of triumphant song.*
*Sing on, sweet singer, till the violets come*
*And south winds blow; sing on, prophetic bird!*
*Oh if my lips, which are for ever dumb,*
*Could sing to men what my sad heart has heard,*
*Life's darkest hour with songs of joy would ring;*
*Life's blackest frost would blossom into spring.*

*Edmond Holmes, 1902*

Ours is a garden in the heart of an urban jungle, a cacophony of colour curving around a concrete crossroads. In summer it is bursting with life; in winter it is a curve of frosted black soil covering secrets aching to be told, life waiting to grow. It hasn't always been so. Once upon a time the strip of earth was nothing more than nothing in inner city Manchester, in Old Trafford to be precise, statistically one of the most deprived areas of the country and known more for its football than its flowers. But when the garden grew there, it became a life-saver.

When I was a small child, in that particular patch of the city, nothing much grew – especially not in winter. The urban jungle had veins and sinews made of metal. Instead of soil, a bed of concrete. Instead of the sound of birds, the swarm of traffic. Instead of the sweet smell of flowers, the stench of smog.

The earth was covered in coldness, which stretched itself over our lives like a dull, thumping headache. My mother had slumped into a pit of depression, lying in bed with the curtains closed even in the middle of the day. I seemed to absorb the mood, mirroring the melancholy overcast sky, which sent sheets of rain hammering into the grey ground.

Nothing seemed to grow. Life seemed to be stuck, stuttering, at an end.

Now I begin to remember how the garden first grew around our house in the heart of the city, how something began to flourish out of nothing, amidst the screech of sirens and honking of horns. Memory begins to bloom in the mind, fertile now to receive it.

One day my mother is not in her usual place in bed. She is outside. She has begun cultivating the garden. Where once there was a concrete strip fringing the house, leading to the blaring crossroads, now there is rich black soil, thick black like my own hair, dark black, blacker than I have ever seen, a beautiful blackness.

The soil smells rich and deep. The soil smells of secrets. I help my mother, or just play in the newly becoming garden. At first there is not much to look at but that soil and the many mysteries within it – a whole new terrain of textures for the young senses. A fat pink worm squirms out of the earth and I scream as its flesh touches my flesh, at its squelchiness, its aliveness. I look over at Mum and her hair is almost camouflaged in blackness – it is a colour which likes us, which is like us, the colour of soil. I peer closely at all the other colours I had seen every day but not really looked at, inspecting the brown bark of the trees, a different brown from our skin, a paler wooden brown, but still brown, with swirling patterns like the patterns on a palm. The brown and black colours of the body which I had been teased about by the boy in the street, by the girl in school, called 'Paki', here in the garden I can see they too are a natural part of the world.

I am no longer apart from, but a part of, the earth.

Cultivating our garden was also a process of cultivating a deeper and richer sense of self, a sense of calm in the self, of comfort in the skin, a greater understanding of a connection with the earth, even here in the heart of the inner city.

The next task is the planting of the bulbs. Mum wears thin garden gloves to touch the soil as she digs a space for the bulbs, tunnelling away into the earth, burrowing out a home for those bulbs, deep enough for each bulb to be safe, for life to grow. She spends long hours in the new garden, passing her sadness away into the soil.

I touch the new earth with my bare hands and the tickle of soil against my skin makes me feel alive. I have not heard my own laughter for a long, long time; I have forgotten the sound. The sound bubbles up as if from deep within, deep within the core of the earth, as if this tunnelling through the earth was bringing out new depths in our own selves.

It is hard to imagine that the bulbs – small, oval-shaped, colourless – will one day sprout a shock of life, will one day flower. I soon forget about them there, but the planting of the bulbs has planted new emotions – the small but potent sense of anticipation, of something to look forward to. It will be some months before the bulbs burst forth, as it takes time for things to grow, Mum explains.

Now there is a small seed planted in the barren earth, of something new: hope. There is a small bulb of expectation in the heart, of waiting for something beautiful to burst open.

*Plant new worlds, quickly, quickly, before the light fades.*

It was lucky that we planted the bulbs when we did, for if we had left it a few days longer the earth would have been too hard for humble human fingers to interfere with. That soft soil would have grown solid and rocky, impenetrable.

It was lucky that we planted the bulbs when we did for just a few days later it became too cold to stay outside for very long at all – seconds even and the breath came out in curling white smoke, the body shivered and the teeth chattered. Winter was intent on making itself known.

It was lucky we planted the bulbs when we did for that winter was one of the longest on record, beginning even in the autumn. The frost clung fiercely, as if tightening its grip, clutching our skulls so that the journey to school was painful in the cold, wind lashing against the skin, pulling tears out of the eyes.

*Plant new worlds, quickly, quickly, before the light fades.*

How does a garden grow? How does anything grow at all? How does something grow from nothing? Growth was a topic very much on the mind during those dark days. Inside the house, there were biro lines etched onto the white wallpaper in the living room monitoring our own growth, as we inched taller.

Deep inside the earth, something was growing, too, something was coming into being, cells were dividing, multiplying, preparing.

All through the cold days, those small bulbs gave me something to imagine. Something to hold on to. I thought about them growing and imagined what kind of colours they might bring forth from the darkness. When still the winter did not melt away into spring, I began to draw paintings of an imaginary garden – gardens of the mind. I drew rich deep black soil, brown bark and then painted layers of bright tulips, roses, daffodils, plum and apple trees and bumble-bees. I painted paths stretching from houses, when I had just learnt the magic of 3D, paths leading into futures that could be dreamed about, in the new space being created for dreams. My imagined garden kept me going, growing through the dark days. It kept the inner space rich and fertile.

The days passed, and the light in the sky began to linger longer. It was harder to have a sense of the light, in a place where the sky was so often overcast, so leaden grey even at the best of times, but the light began to pierce down in sudden sharp, brief rays, before vanishing.

And then one morning, an astonishment of golden yellow in the black, golden yellow in the black, a daffodil burst open. I stepped out to go to school, sleep still crusted in the eyes, heavy lids from a night of restlessness filled with troubled dreams as usual – the joyriders had started screeching up and down the road at all hours, so there was no peace in that house in the city. There was no quiet. That first daffodil woke me clean out of slumber, scraped sleep away, washed away weariness and I breathed deeply in astonishment at the new life just outside our house, the first thing to have grown in the garden. I gazed long and deep at the daffodil so that I could carry it inside the mind once I had left to go to school – and throughout the grey day at school, the daffodil bloomed within. I loved the daffodil.

Here was colour all the darkness in the world could not wash away.

Soon after that, there was no stopping our garden. The tulips burst open in a shock of red, howling out with life. The roses grew from the bush. Flowers I didn't know the name of sprang forth, purple ones and pink ones crowded together in a panic of colour. Then the fruit grew thick and the plums splashed to the floor and burst open. My siblings and I started a plum business, selling plums for 2p to passers-by. Once there was an unpleasant incident as a passerby took a plum and threw it at me: 'I wouldn't buy plums from a Paki,' he spat. But where once the words would have crushed, would have stung, now a greater bedrock of strength had been planted within.

The world burst open in colour and sweet scent and light. The deep depression that had burrowed its way into the bones and hearts of the humans of the house was lifted and lightened, for now.

It wasn't only the bulbs that had been purposefully planted that were enchanting, but the accidental growths. For even among the rubble and concrete, even among the litter and debris, the tip of discarded dreams, can something grow. Life grows in places you least expect it; the dandelion springs in an astonishment of colour between the gaps in the grey pavement. Its delicate body was battered by the weather, for it was born in an unfortunate location and it was pounded by rain, fierce, and whipped by winds, ferocious, so it would sway and bow and bend in the wind but still it did not die. It blazed briefly, that flower, so that all who passed along the path, the concrete roadside, on the otherwise forlorn day, so that all who passed through this wasteland could glance down and should they chance to see it perhaps their hearts too would bloom and fill with a sudden moment of joy.

The garden was a fresh start, quite literally – the possibility and palpability of new beginnings. I knew it wouldn't last, the glory of the garden in full bloom. So when the leaves started to fall and the flower petals curled and wilted, and the sweet scents evaporated to leave the smog, and the birds stopped singing and migrated to Africa, I didn't entirely despair. I knew this was the rhythm of the earth.

I knew it would happen again, the opening up of the world. Our garden had given me hope.

It is now two decades after that first planting, and the winter is a cold one this year, one of the longest winters on record, the cold and dark burrowing its way into the bones. I am alone and far away from home, but that forgotten first garden is growing within. Now I am remembering that garden in the midst of the urban jungle, and how it held gold in the dark. For a long time it had been buried beneath darker memories, but now it is growing within me, its roots and its branches, its soft, fierce soil, its determination to grow, where growth was least expected. Now I feel anew its ferocity of life-force, a thing of beauty yearning to grow, despite everything.

*Anita Sethi, 2016*

Every year, in the third week of February, there is a day, or, more usually, a run of days, when one can say for sure that the light is back. Some juncture has been reached, and the light spills into the world from a sun suddenly higher in the sky. Today, a Sunday, is such a day, though the trees are still stark and without leaves; the grasses are dry and winter-beaten.

The sun is still low in the sky, even at noon, hanging over the hills southwest. Its light spills out of the southwest, the same direction as the wind: both sunlight and wind arrive together out of the same airt, an invasion of light and air out of a sky of quickly moving clouds, working together as a swift team. The wind lifts the grasses and moves the thin branches of the leafless trees and the sun shines on them, in one movement, so light and air are as one, two aspects of the same entity. The light is razor-like, edging grasses and twigs of the willow and apple trees and birch. The garden is all left-leaning filaments of light, such as you see on cobwebs, mostly, too hard to be called a sparkle, too metallic, but the whole garden's being given a brisk spring-clean. Where there are leaves, such as the holly 200 yards away, the wind lifts the leaves and the sun sweeps underneath. All moving because of the fresh wind.

Now the town's jackdaws are all up in a crowd, revelling in the wind, chack-chacking at each other. And I hear a girl's voice, one of my daughter's friends, one of the four girls playing in the garden. She makes a call poised just between play and fear. What are they playing? Hide and seek? No matter. It pleases me that my daughter says they are 'playing in the garden', because they're eleven years old; another year or two and they wouldn't admit to 'playing' at all, and for a while the garden will have no appeal, because everything they want will be elsewhere. For a few years they'll enter a dark mirror-tunnel whose sides reflect only themselves.

The girls themselves can't be seen, obscured by trees and that edgy, breezy light. The year has turned. Filaments and metallic ribbons of wind-blown light, just for an hour, but enough.

*Kathleen Jamie,* Sightlines, *2012*

# Author Biographies

**Nick Acheson** grew up in wellies, watching bog bush-crickets in North Norfolk. A year spent in the Camargue during his degree inspired him to seek wilder landscapes and for ten glorious years he lived in Bolivia. Since returning to the UK he has worked the world over, from Arctic tundras to the Antarctic. He proudly works closely with Norfolk Wildlife Trust, for whom he regularly features in local press and media.

**Jane Adams** grew up in an overcrowded London suburb with an unexplained love of all things wild. It took forty years before her passion properly surfaced after moving to an old house on the south coast with a rambling, wild garden. Now a self-confessed middle-aged wildlife nerd, her interests include photography, social media, writing, trail running and nature conservation. @wildlifestuff

**Richard Adams** is most famous as the author of *Watership Down*, as well as many other international bestsellers, most of which reflect his fascination with and love for nature. He lives in Hampshire.

**Joseph Addison** (d. 1719) was a writer and politician. He was a well-known essayist, contributing 247 to the daily publication *The Spectator*, which he co-founded in 1711, as well as writing several poems and plays.

**Al Alvarez** is a writer, poet and critic. He was the poetry editor and critic at the *Observer* from 1956–66 and his books include *The Savage God* (2002), *Feeding the Rat* (2003) and *Pondlife* (2013).

**Sophie Bagshaw** is an 18-year-old all-round naturalist, starting to learn the tricks of the trade in ecology. She likes walking around local, secret patches and seeing the changes in biodiversity over the changing seasons. One of her main interests is beachcombing along the river banks and beaches collecting washed-up treasures.

**Jacqueline Bain** lives in Paisley, Scotland. She is a former nurse, unable to work due to extensive knee surgery. She enjoys writing fiction and non-fiction in which nature will always feature somewhere. Her main hobbies include bird watching and creating space and homes in the garden for mini-beasts, in between throwing a ball for Bonny, her fourteen-year-old Border collie.

**Anna Laetitia Barbauld** (d. 1825) was a poet and children's author, one of the few successful female writers at the time. Her literary career came to an end in 1812 after her poem *Eighteen Hundred and Eleven* attracted fierce criticism for her negative views of the British Empire and its role in the Napoleonic Wars.

**Wilhelm Nero Pilate Barbellion** was the pseudonym under which Bruce Frederick Cummings (d. 1919) published *The Diary of a Disappointed Man* after discovering he was suffering from multiple sclerosis and only had a short time to live. Described as one of the most moving diaries ever written, it recorded his reflections on nature and on both the brevity and the beauty of life.

**Patrick Barkham** writes for the *Guardian* and is the author of *The Butterfly Isles* (2010), *Badgerlands* (2013) and *Coastlines* (2015). His next book, *Islander*, is an exploration of Britain's small islands and will be published in 2017. He lives in Norfolk.

**Julian Beach**, originally from Staffordshire and now in Laugharne, Wales, returned to writing after a two-decade estrangement from the muse. He is currently applying the finishing touches to 'The Needwood Poems', inspired by memories of growing up in the ancient Needwood Forest, most of which fell to the encloser's axe in the nineteenth century. He blogs at: julianbeachwriting.wordpress.com.

**Adrian Bell** (d. 1980) was a Suffolk farmer and journalist who wrote over twenty-five ruralist books, including *Corduroy* (1930) *Silver Ley* (1931) and *The Cherry Tree* (1932), which together form his farm trilogy. He was the first person to compile the now legendary *Times* crossword, setting over 5,000 puzzles and helping to develop the cryptic clue style.

**Liz Berry** is a poet whose work has been published in numerous magazines and anthologies. Her debut collection, *Black Country* (2014), was a Poetry Book Society Recommendation and also won a Somerset Maugham Award, the Geoffrey Faber Memorial Award and the Forward Prize for Best First Collection 2014. You can hear Liz read her own work at: www.poetryarchive.org/poet/liz-berry

**Kate Blincoe** is a nature-loving mother of two and freelance writer for publications such as the *Guardian*. She is the author of *The No-Nonsense Guide to Green Parenting* and is never happier than when exploring the countryside with her family.

**Ronald Blythe** is the author of more than twenty books, most famously *Aken-field: Portrait of an English Village* (1969), a fictionalised account of a Suffolk village from 1890 to 1966, which became the record of ways of rural life that were rapidly vanishing from Britain. He is also the author of the much-loved and long running 'Words from Wormingford' column in the *Church Times*.

**Nicholas Breton** (d. 1626) was a prolific writer of religious and pastoral poems, satires and prose works. Little concrete detail is known about his life, but he was well regarded as an author in his lifetime, although forgotten quickly afterwards. His final book, *Fantasticks* (1626), offers great insight into the customs of the era.

**Brian Carter** (d. 2015) was a Devon-based author, artist and conservation columnist with a deep affection for the landscape and wildlife of his home county. Many of his writings featured his beloved Dartmoor as backdrop, including *A Black Fox Running* (1981) and *Jack: A Novel* (1986).

**Nicola Chester** writes about the wildlife she finds wherever she is, mostly roaming the North Wessex Downs, where she lives with her husband and three children. She has written professionally for over a decade. Nicola is particularly passionate about engaging people with nature and how language can communicate the thrill of wild experiences. You can read her blog here: nicolachester.wordpress.com

**John Clare** (d. 1864) was the son of a farm labourer who went on to produce some of English poetry's best works on the countryside, rural life and nature. Known as The Northamptonshire Peasant Poet in his time, a sense of alienation and disruption became themes of his work, such as 'I Am' (1848).

**Jack Clemo** (d. 1994) was a writer from Cornwall. His debut novel, *Wilding Graft* (1948), won an Atlantic Award, and he went on to write several collections of poetry, including *The Clay Verge* (1951) and *The Map of Clay* (1961). His work often featured and was inspired by the Cornish scenery.

**Hartley Coleridge** was the eldest son of Samuel Taylor Coleridge. A poet, biographer and teacher, he was a familiar figure in the countryside of the Lake District, where he lived for most of his life.

**Samuel Taylor Coleridge** (d. 1834) was a poet, literary critic and philosopher whose joint publication with William Wordsworth, *Lyrical Ballads* (1798), is credited with marking the beginning of the Romantic period in English poetry. A member of the Lake Poets, some of his most famous works include 'The Rime of the Ancient Mariner' (1798) and 'Kubla Khan' (1816).

**Roger Deakin** (d. 2006) is best known for his book *Waterlog* (1999), which documented his experiences of wild swimming across Britain. His subsequent books *Wildwood* (2007) and *Notes from Walnut Farm* (2008) were published posthumously to great acclaim.

**Charles Dickens** (d. 1870) is one of Britain's most famous and best-loved novelists. Besides establishing, editing and writing for two weekly publications, *Household Words* (1850–9) and *All The Year Round* (1859–70) and campaigning tirelessly for social justice and reform, he also wrote fourteen novels, including *Oliver Twist* (1837–9), *A Tale of Two Cities* (1859) and *Great Expectations* (1861).

**Jon Dunn** is a natural history writer, photographer and wildlife tour leader based in the Shetland Isles. Author of *Britain's Sea Mammals*, his work takes him throughout Europe and the Americas. Once stalked by a mountain lion while birding on the edge of Mexico's Sierra Madre Occidental, he generally prefers experiencing wildlife on his own terms and not as part of the food chain. www.jondunn.com

**Olaudah Equiano** (d. 1797) was a freed slave from Africa who settled in London in 1767 after travelling from America, and became an active supporter of the abolition of the slave trade. In 1780 his autobiography *The Interesting Narrative of the Life of Olaudah Equiano* was published, an important and influential work that recounted the horrific experience of his enslavement.

**Kristian Evans** is from Kenfig, Wales. Interested particularly in ecology and local history and the history of magic, he writes an online journal for the environmental charity Sustainable Wales. His ongoing research installation 'The Mirror's Grain' was launched at Kenfig National Nature Reserve in 2010. A pamphlet of poems, 'Unleaving', was published by HappenStance Press in 2015.

**Thomas Furly Forster** (d. 1825) was a botanist who compiled many lists and drawings of plants. After his death, his natural history journals were collated and published by his son as *The Pocket Encyclopaedia of Natural Phenomena*.

**Chris Foster** is a birdwatcher, gradually evolving into an all-round naturalist, based in Reading, Berkshire. On top of teaching associate and PhD positions at Reading University, Chris is an aspiring nature writer supported by A Focus On Nature, the youth conservation network. His wildlife blog is entering its sixth year; his work has also appeared in *Biosphere* and *Antenna* magazines.

**John Fowles** (d. 2005) was a novelist of international repute whose many popular works included *The Collector* (1963), *The Magus* (1965) and *The French Lieu-*

*tenant's Woman* (1969). His books have been translated in many countries and several were also adapted for the screen.

**Tiffany Francis** is a nature writer and wildlife illustrator living in the South Downs, Hampshire. Her first book on foraging will be published by Bloomsbury in spring 2018, and she hopes to pursue a PhD in Environmental Literature in the near future. She likes mammals, sloe gin and offensive cheese.

**Elizabeth Gardiner** (d. 2010) lived in a Wiltshire hamlet for over thirty years. She was a regular contributor to her local village newsletter, the *Biddestone Broadsheet*, her sparky 'Notes from Giddeahall' giving acute and witty insights into her neighbours, both human and animal, wild and domesticated, throughout the changing seasons. She was a prolific writer of short stories, articles and poetry, much of which remains unpublished.

**Matt Gaw** is a journalist who writes about experiences in nature close to his home in Suffolk. He contributes a monthly wildlife diary to the *Suffolk Magazine* and edits Suffolk Wildlife Trust's membership magazine. You can read his blog here: mattgawjournalist.wordpress.com

**Iain Green** is a wildlife photographer and author who also runs Wildlife Wonder, a social enterprise engaging school children and community groups with the nature on their doorstep. Working with more than 8,000 children a year in schools across the UK, Iain uses creativity, photography and discovery to encourage exploration and enjoyment of the natural world. www.wildlifewonder.co.uk

**Caroline Greville** is writing a book on her involvement with badgers in the context of her family life and wider rural setting. This memoir forms the main part of her PhD at the University of Kent, alongside research into new nature writing. She is Secretary of the East Kent Badger Group and teaches creative writing.

**Sir Edward Grey** (d. 1933) was a Liberal statesman, and the longest serving foreign secretary of the twentieth century (1905–16). He was also a keen ornithologist, and published *The Charm of Birds* in 1927, a record of his observations of birds and their song.

**Elizabeth Guntrip** is a young writer, naturalist and campaigner. She has authored pieces for the BBC, RSPB, Wildfowl & Wetlands Trust and Royal Horticultural Society, among others. She regularly speaks on *Springwatch* and *Autumnwatch* about inclusive access to nature, as well as on independent film and BBC radio. She co-created #WildlifeFromMyWindow with BBC Earth and is an M.E. awareness ambassador. www.lizzieguntrip.co.uk / tweets @lizzieguntrip

**Jen Hadfield** is a poet based in Shetland. She has published three collections of her poetry: *Almanacs* (2005), *Nigh-No-Place* (2008), which won the T. S. Eliot Prize for poetry that year, and *Byssus* (2014).

**Thomas Hardy** (d. 1928) wrote several famous works, including *Far from the Madding Crowd* (1874), *The Mayor of Casterbridge* (1886) and *Tess of the d'Urbervilles* (1891). Rural society was a major theme in his books; most were set in the partly imagined region of Wessex, based largely on areas of south and southwest England.

**Edmond Holmes** (d. 1936) was an Irish poet and educator, who published several books and poetry collections, including *The Triumph of Love* (1903), *The Creed of the Buddha* (1908) and *Sonnets to the Universe* (1918).

**Kathleen Jamie** is a poet and essayist whose writing is inspired by her native Scottish countryside. Her works include *The Tree House* (2004), *The Overhaul* (2012) and *Sightlines* (2012). She has been shortlisted for and won numerous awards, including two Forward Poetry Prizes, Scottish Book of the Year Award, the John Burroughs Medal and the Orion Book Award.

**Richard Jefferies** (d. 1887) was a nature writer of both essays and novels, inspired by his upbringing on a farm. His works include *The Amateur Poacher* (1879), *Round About a Great Estate* (1880), *Nature Near London* (1883) and *The Life of the Fields* (1884). The collection *Field and Hedgerow* was published posthumously in 1889.

**Lucy Jones** is a nature writer and journalist based in London. She is the author of *Foxes Unearthed* and her writing has also been published in *BBC Earth*, *BBC Wildlife*, the *Guardian*, *TIME* and the *New Statesman*. She runs the Wildlife Daily blog, featuring wildlife, nature and environment news from around the world.

**James Joyce** (d. 1941) was an Irish writer best known for his classic novel *Ulysses* (1922). His other notable works include *Dubliners* (1914), *A Portrait of the Artist as a Young Man* (1916) and *Finnegans Wake* (1939).

**Emma Kemp**, tiring of a life of crime, recently gave up practising criminal law to complete a masters in Nature and Travel Writing. She lives in Oxfordshire, not far from the Thames.

**Nakul Krishna** was born in Bangalore, India, and studied for a doctorate in philosophy at Balliol College, Oxford. He now lives in north London and is a lecturer in philosophy at the University of Cambridge.

**Satish Kumar** is Editor Emeritus of *Resurgence* and *Ecologist* magazines. His autobiography, *No Destination*, first published in 1978, has sold over 50,000 copies. He is also the author of *You Are, Therefore I Am, Earth Pilgrim* and *Soil, Soul, Society*. In 2008, as part of BBC2's *Natural World* series, he presented a 50-minute documentary from Dartmoor, which was watched by over 3.6 million people.

**Dr Rob Lambert** is an academic, broadcaster, birder and expedition ship lecturer, based at the University of Nottingham where he teaches and writes about environmental history, eco-tourism and nature–people relationships over time. He holds a Visiting Fellowship at the University of Western Australia, and is Vice-President of the Isles of Scilly Wildlife Trust. On 19 June 2015, Rob saw his 500th species of bird in the UK: a Cretzschmar's bunting on Bardsey Island.

**Mary Leapor** (d. 1746) was a poet who died at the age of 24 and was unrecognised during her lifetime. A friend arranged the publication of her work posthumously, in *Poems Upon Several Occasions* (1748).

**Clare Leighton** (d. 1989) was an artist, writer and illustrator famous for her work depicting scenes of rural life. Her best-known works include *The Farmer's Year: A Calendar of English Husbandry* (1933) and *Four Hedges: A Gardener's Chronicle* (1935).

**Andrea Levy** began writing in her mid-thirties, driven by the lack of black voices in English literature. Her fourth book, *Small Island* (2004), garnered her first major critical success, winning the Orange Prize for Fiction and later being adapted for television, followed by Man Booker-nominated *The Long Song* (2011). Her writing often touches on themes of cultural identity and displacement.

**Ann MacCarthy** lives in the Peak District and has supported the work of the Derbyshire Wildlife Trust for many years. She considers a fine day spent indoors to be wasted, preferring to be out in the hills, observing the wildlife and environment of the local moorlands. She is interested in nature writing, landscape and wildlife photography.

**Robert Macfarlane** is an award-winning author whose works include *Mountains of the Mind* (2003), *The Wild Places* (2007), *The Old Ways* (2012) and *Landmarks* (2015). His writing has appeared in numerous publications including the *Guardian*, the *Sunday Times* and the *New York Times*.

**Louis MacNeice** (d. 1963) was an Irish poet and playright who was part of the Auden Group. His works include *The Earth Compels* (1938), *Autumn Journal* (1939), *Christopher Columbus* (1944) and *The Dark Tower* (1946).

**Christina McLeish** is writing a book about exile and Englishness. Born and raised in Melbourne, she came to Cambridge to read for a PhD in the philosophy of science, during which she fell in love with birds and the English countryside. In autumn 2016, after fifteen years, she lost her right to live in England and had to return to Australia.

**Lucy McRobert** is the Nature Matters campaigns manager for The Wildlife Trusts. She has written for publications including *BBC Wildlife*, is a columnist for *Birdwatch* magazine and was the Researcher on Tony Juniper's *What Nature Does for Britain* (2015). She is the creative director of A Focus On Nature, the youth nature network, and is a keen birdwatcher and mammal-watcher.

**David North** has been interested in wildlife and wild places as long as he can remember and he has worked for National Trust, RSPB and for the last ten years at Norfolk Wildlife Trust. He lives in North Norfolk with his wife Tasha and at weekends can be found exploring the local coast between Cley Marshes and Salthouse.

**Eleanor Parker** is a historian and writer, with a doctorate in medieval English literature from the University of Oxford. Her research focuses on historical narratives in literature produced in England between *c.*1000 and *c.*1400.

**Matt Poacher** is learning (slowly) to be an English teacher. When he's not doing that he's either screaming into the wind, or looking for badgers. Often both at the same time. He's written for *The Wire*, *Mojo* and Caught by the River and has a website at www.somesmallcorner.co.uk

**Bethany Pope** has written several collections of poetry: *A Radiance* (2012), *Crown of Thorns* (2013) and *The Gospel of Flies* (2014), *Undisturbed Circles* (2014), and *The Rag and Boneyard* (Indigo Dreams, 2016). Her first novel, *Masque*, was published in 2016.

**Jini Reddy** has written widely for national newspapers and magazines. Born in Britain and raised in Quebec, she is now based in London. Her first book, *Wild Times*, was published in 2016.

**Anita Sethi** is a journalist, writer and critic whose work has appeared in the *Guardian* and *Observer*, *Granta*, and on BBC radio among other outlets. She is recipient of a Penguin/decibel prize, has been published in several anthologies and is currently completing a book. She was born in Manchester. www.anitasethi.co.uk / @anitasethi

**William Shakespeare** (d. 1616) was one of the world's greatest writers. He wrote about 154 sonnets and 38 plays, including *Romeo and Juliet, Hamlet* and *Macbeth*, which continue to be studied, performed and adapted all over the world. His sonnets were published in 1609 but are believed to have been composed earlier.

**Edward Step** (d. 1931) was the author of numerous books on nature, both popular and specialist, including *Favourite Flowers of the Garden and Greenhouse* (1896), *The Romance of Wild Flowers* (1901), *Nature in the Garden* (1910) and *Nature Rambles: An Introduction to Country-lore* (1930).

**Robert Louis Stevenson** (d. 1894) was a Scottish writer and one of the most celebrated writers of his time. His most famous works include *Treasure Island* (1883), *Kidnapped* (1886) and *Strange Case of Dr Jekyll and Mr Hyde* (1886).

**Sheila Stewart** (d. 2014) wrote several books depicting the lives of working people in rural areas based on extensive interviews with her subjects, including *A Home from Home* (1967), *Country Kate* (1971), *Lifting the Latch: A Life on the Land* (1987) and *Ramlin Rose: The Boatwoman's Story* (1994).

**Henry Tegner** (d. 1977) wrote extensively on the wildlife in the north of England. His books include *The Roe Deer: Their History, Habits and Pursuit* (1951), *The White Foxes of Gorfenletch* (1954) and *A Border County: Being an Account of its Wild Life and Field Sports* (1955).

**R. S. Thomas** (d. 2000) was a Welsh poet and priest. Having already published three collections of poetry, his breakthrough came with his fourth volume, *Song at the Year's Turning* (1955), which won the Royal Society of Literature's Heinemann Award. He also won the 1964 Queen's Gold Medal for poetry in 1964, and in 1996 he was nominated for the Nobel Prize in Literature.

**Claire Thurlow** grew up in Kent but now lives in rural Hampshire. She is a freelance writer and leads creative writing workshops for people who write for pleasure and well-being. When not wandering the countryside with notebook and camera, she's at her desk working on her first novel.

**Reverend Gilbert White** (d. 1793) was a curate, as well as a keen naturalist and ornithologist. His best known work is *The Natural History and Antiquities of Sel-*

*borne* (1789); his journals were published posthumously, in 1931. He is considered by many to have been a major influence in forming modern attitudes to and respect for nature.

**Henry Williamson** (d. 1977) was an English naturalist and writer. His most famous novel was *Tarka the Otter* (1928), which won the Hawthornden Prize for literature. He also wrote several books on natural history, including *The Story of a Norfolk Farm* (1941), and his experiences during the First World War, such as *The Wet Flanders Plain* (1929).

**Janet Willoner** lives in North Yorkshire and has been passionate about nature since childhood. She studied and taught Natural Sciences, had a career as a landscape watercolourist and took up writing on retirement. She has always loved spending time in wild places, experiencing solitude and observing wildlife, all of which inspire her art and writing.

**Virginia Woolf** (d. 1941) was one of the great writers of the twentieth century. A modernist and one of the key figures of the Bloomsbury Group, her most famous novels include *Mrs Dalloway* (1925), *Orlando* (1928) and *To the Lighthouse* (1927).

**William Wordsworth** (d. 1850) was one of England's greatest Romantic poets, creating some of the most famous poems in the English language, including 'I Wandered Lonely as a Cloud'. What is often considered his greatest work, *The Prelude* (previously known as the 'poem to Coleridge'), was published posthumously. Wordsworth was Poet Laureate from 1843 until his death.

**Annie Worsley** is a mother of four and grandmother living on a coastal croft in the remote Northwest Highlands of Scotland. A former academic who explored the relationships between humans and environments in diverse parts of the world, including Papua New Guinea, she now writes about nature, wildlife and landscape. She tries to paint the wild using words.

## ALSO AVAILABLE IN THIS SERIES

The Seasons books aim to capture the changing year through evocative pieces of writing about nature, describing the life-cycles of flora and fauna, startling moments of transition, seasonal change in cities and gardens, and wildlife experiences that epitomise a point in the year or the shifting patterns of country life.

Each book includes a collection of writing, old and new – extracts from classic texts, lesser-known historical material, new works from established nature writers and some pieces by Wildlife Trusts supporters throughout the UK – threaded together to mirror the unfolding of the seasons.

*Spring*
978-1-78396-223-5

*Summer*
978-1-78396-244-0

*Autumn*
978-1-78396-248-8